"To live in our true God-given i[dentity]
we are each fearfully and wonde[rfully]
He gave us our emotions as a gift [and]
them lead in our attitudes, decisio[ns]
from God's truth. Increased confidence, enduring peace, and lasting
calm will be the by-products when readers learn to acknowledge and
better manage their emotions (instead of allowing their emotions to
manage them). The truths gleaned from *Emotional Confidence* will
reduce their stress, improve their ability to make rational decisions,
and deepen their relationship with God. Make the investment in your
own mental and emotional well-being, as you discover who God truly
created you to be."

Michelle Bengtson, PhD, board certified clinical
neuropsychologist, podcast host, and award-winning author

"If you want to manage your emotions while glorifying the Lord,
then this book is for you. Through mindful reflections, biblical insight, and her own expertise, Alicia gives us the tools we need to
break free from our negative thought patterns and walk in emotional
confidence!"

Nicole Jacobsmeyer, author of *Take Back Your Joy*

"In a world filled with chaos and uncertainty, Alicia Michelle's *Emotional Confidence* is a beacon of hope and guidance for those seeking
peace amid the storm. This transformative book provides a refreshing
approach to emotional management, blending biblical wisdom with
practical strategies to navigate life's ups and downs with grace and
clarity. I wholeheartedly endorse this book as a must-read for anyone
longing for emotional freedom and spiritual clarity."

Shayna Rattler, founder of A God Shift

"*Emotional Confidence* is a game changer for anyone burdened by
toxic emotions. Alicia Michelle's ADD method offers a transformative path for Christians to process emotions in a way that honors
Christ and brings true healing. If you're seeking genuine freedom
in your mental and emotional well-being, this book is an absolute
must-read."

Carlie Kercheval, MA, Christian counselor, certified life
breakthrough coach, and founder of Wives of Integrity®

"I don't know if anyone wakes up thinking, *I want to grow in emotional confidence*, but we all should! Alicia Michelle unpacks what's
at stake if we don't process our negative emotions and describes the
vibrant life that awaits us if we do. If you've ever dealt with trauma,
loneliness, anger, disappointment, or relentless stress, you need this

book. *Emotional Confidence* gives us a relatable, practical, and biblical way forward."

Becky Keife, author of several books, including
Create in Me a Heart of Peace and *The Simple Difference*

"Alicia tackles the tricky topic of emotions and emotional health in an engaging and easy-to-apply format. Using biblical truth, she helps us make sense of the emotional jumble within to find peace and calm in the chaos of life. This comprehensive resource offers an abundance of practical tools, thoughtful questions, and helpful suggestions to help navigate our inner worlds."

Heather Creekmore, podcast host and bestselling author of
The 40-Day Body Image Workbook

"Are you frustrated because what you hear about controlling your emotions isn't working? Alicia Michelle writes with understanding from her own emotional struggles. This perfectly timed book will help us break free from frustrating emotional cycles by teaching the best strategies for lasting change."

Sarah Geringer, editor, book launch manager, podcast host,
artist, and author of *Hope for the Hard Days*

"At times, our emotions can feel overwhelming and unsettling. Alicia will help us learn mindset life skills that honor the validity of our emotions while simultaneously reverencing God's truth. In this profound book, she combines science and Scripture, showing us how to live the abundant life God promised with emotional confidence. I highly recommend!"

Becky Harling, international conference speaker,
John Maxwell certified coach, and bestselling author of
How to Listen So People Will Talk

"Alicia Michelle has written a lifeline of practical, biblical help and hope to rescue and redeem us in the vast sea of our God-given emotions."

Pam Farrel, author of several books, including bestselling
Men Are Like Waffles—Women Are Like Spaghetti and
10 Best Decisions a Single Mom Can Make

"Refreshing. Thorough. Didactic. Inspirational. Hope-infused. I devoured the profound truths Alicia Michelle shares in *Emotional Confidence*. I love the way she beautifully comes alongside as a guide and friend, cheering us on with honesty and vulnerability while bathing all she says in love. This practical guidebook is a powerful resource if you're ready to move toward wholehearted freedom."

Michelle Watson Canfield, PhD, LPC, author of
Let's Talk and host of *The Dad Whisperer Podcast*

Emotional
CONFIDENCE

Emotional CONFIDENCE

3 SIMPLE STEPS TO MANAGE EMOTIONS WITH SCIENCE AND SCRIPTURE

ALICIA MICHELLE, ACC, CPLC

BakerBooks

a division of Baker Publishing Group
Grand Rapids, Michigan

Published by Baker Books
a division of Baker Publishing Group
Grand Rapids, Michigan
BakerBooks.com

Printed in the United States of America

Library of Congress Cataloging-in-Publication Data
Names: Michelle, Alicia, 1975– author.
Title: Emotional confidence : 3 simple steps to manage emotions with science and
   scripture / Alicia Michelle, ACC, CPLC.
Description: Grand Rapids, Michigan : Baker Books, a division of Baker Publishing
   Group, [2024] | Includes bibliographical references.
Identifiers: LCCN 2024005417 | ISBN 9781540904027 (paperback) | ISBN
   9781540904522 (casebound) | ISBN 9781493447046 (ebook)
Subjects: LCSH: Emotions—Religious aspects—Christianity. | Confidence—
   Religious aspects—Christianity. | Decision making—Religious
   aspects—Christianity.
Classification: LCC BV4597.3 .M534 2024 | DDC 152.4—dc23/eng/20240506
LC record available at https://lccn.loc.gov/2024005417

Cover design by Mumtaz Mustafa

The author is represented by the literary agency of WordServe Literary Group, www .wordserveliterary.com.

Baker Publishing Group publications use paper produced from sustainable forestry practices and postconsumer waste whenever possible.

24   25   26   27   28   29   30   7   6   5   4   3   2

To the one who always says yes
to my wild ideas and supports me in every way.

I love you always and forever.

Contents

Introduction

As a highly sensitive person who wears her emotions on her sleeve—and subsequently has the world's worst poker face—this is the book I've personally needed but could never find.

I was the emotional teenager who locked herself in her room and cried uncontrollably; the exhausted young mom who felt emotionally run over by motherhood's relentless demands; and the driven, perfectionist workaholic who defined her worth and her emotional status by what she had or had not accomplished in a day.

For the longest time my feelings ruled my life, which left me guilty, ashamed, and a bit dizzy from the emotional roller coaster. I was sure that Jesus was disappointed in this girl who couldn't seem to manage all the inner turmoil when everyone else seemed so emotionally content and in control of themselves. (Spoiler alert: you know most people stuff their emotions and put on a happy face too, right?)

I needed someone to teach me *how* to manage uncomfortable emotions, not to just give me Bible verses about why certain emotions were wrong.

I needed a practical way to talk myself through my emotions without accepting every feeling as fact or instantly judging myself for having that feeling.

Does this resonate with you? If so, you're in the right place. When it comes to managing emotions, this book is all about practical how-tos instead of pat answers.

As a trained and ICF-certified Christian mindset coach, I don't believe we need to ditch our feelings and just focus on truth like some people preach. Nor do I believe we should indulge all our feelings and let our emotions be our ultimate guide, like others advise.

In these pages we'll explore the happy medium of managing emotions using scientific research and Scripture. While God's Word is supreme over all things, both emotions and biblical truth play an important role in allowing us to understand ourselves and our reactions.

Not only does God give us the ability to feel and to express ourselves, He also cares about what matters to us because we matter to Him. While He won't always remove us from painful situations, He will stand with us in the turmoil and help us find our way to the other side.

About Emotional Confidence

Maybe you're wondering, *What exactly is emotional confidence?* You won't find the phrase defined in a psychology textbook or academic lecture. *Emotional confidence* is a term I've coined after experiencing my own emotional metamorphosis and working with hundreds of Christian women to help them cultivate their own emotional peace. Here's my definition:

> Emotional confidence is the inner certainty to wholly recognize and honestly process all that one feels with God's compassion, clarity, and courage.

To use poetic metaphor, emotional confidence is an ongoing dance of curiosity as we acknowledge our ever-changing emotional state through the wise, compassionate gaze of our loving God. It's a sacred assurance of believing that our emotions have purpose and that our Savior Himself wants to partner with us to better understand what we're feeling. It's the joy of knowing that no emotion is too big or too frightening to process when we decide to seek His courage to respond for His glory and our good.

Being emotionally confident doesn't mean we're exempt from experiencing the frustrating emotions found in the darkest, most difficult life circumstances. It just means that we have coping tools, practical strategies, and, most importantly, the Holy Spirit as our seasoned guide to help us through the hard places.

In these pages we'll unpack an emotional management tool I've developed called *ADD* (acknowledge, discern, decide) that has helped tens of thousands effectively navigate painful emotions. Whether teaching ADD in a one-on-one coaching session, in a podcast episode, or to a large conference audience, I've seen firsthand how this simple three-part process has the power to radically change how we relate to ourselves, our circumstances, and our loved ones.

My ultimate hope is that through these pages you'll uncover the hidden treasure of knowing God as your emotional partner. Not even our deepest shame or our most hate-filled feelings can keep Him from wanting to work with us to discover emotional healing. He wants to be that voice of compassion, clarity, and courage as we wrestle with the good, bad, and ugly aspects of human emotion.

Jesus is the compassionate, wisdom-filled, courage-instilling Lord who will use all things, including the most painful emotions, to draw us closer to Him.

As you let down your guard and welcome God into the messy, unkempt places of your heart, may He prove Himself a safe hiding place to process all your joys and sorrows.

Cheering for you,

Alicia

Mental Health Statement

Working through our feelings can certainly feel overwhelming and messy, and it's impossible for me to know where you are emotionally as you read through these pages. As you might expect from a book on managing feelings, we do mention potentially emotionally triggering topics. I apologize in advance if this adds to any mental suffering you may be experiencing, as that is not my intention.

If you feel that you need additional help processing your emotions—especially those related to any form of trauma—please seek the help of a mental health professional. If you are in the United States, Focus on the Family and the American Association of Christian Counselors have Christian mental health recommendations on their sites. Your pastor may also be able to recommend some trusted Christian counselors in your area.

Don't wait to get help. If you are suffering from emotional abuse or any other form of abuse, please remove yourself from the situation and contact the proper authorities as needed.

In addition, should you ever feel that your emotions may cause you to harm yourself or others, please seek help from emergency resources in your area.

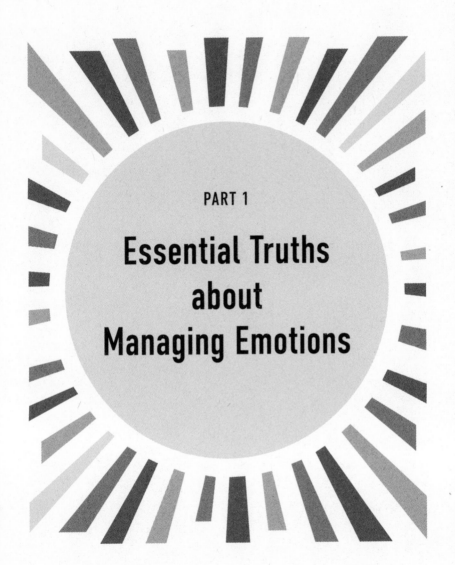

PART 1

Essential Truths about Managing Emotions

1

The Cost of Hiding, Stuffing, and Running from Our Emotions

Kate Bowler was especially emotional the morning she secretly left her hospital room and marched downstairs to the gift shop.

Dressed in her blue hospital gown, with an IV strapped to her arm, Kate found herself in the back of the store, angrily ripping self-help books off a neatly curated endcap, much to the confusion of the gift shop staff.

As she picked up each book and verbally berated it, Kate tearfully explained to the bewildered clerk and her manager that these hope-filled titles with their positive, can-do Christian rhetoric shouldn't share the same airspace as stillborn children and incurable diseases.

What the store personnel didn't know was that Kate had just learned she had stage IV colon cancer.[1]

Whether it's a life-altering diagnosis or the everyday stress of living with imperfect people in a highly uncertain world, difficult emotions seem like bulky, unfair obstacles hindering us from what feels like our God-given right to peace and happiness.

As Christians we know our hope is not in this world, and we're called to keep our eyes on Jesus as our source of joy. Even so, life is hard, and problems are everywhere! We are tragically flawed humans living in fleshly bodies surrounded by dysfunctional relationships, unpredictable circumstances, and all kinds of unsolvable dilemmas. Painful emotions are inevitable, and they can leave us feeling at war with the freedom promised to us in Christ.

Many of us have found success in careers or relationships but can't seem to manage our feelings. Emotions can feel like a mysterious, confusing no-man's-land—like a slippery ball we're thrown but can't ever catch. We wonder what to do with our tumultuous feelings, especially when they complicate relationships, sway important decisions, and lead us to live quite contrary to how God wants us to as Christ followers. When should we express our emotions and when should we silence them?

Taking it further, many of us have a bigger question: *how* are we supposed to navigate the confusing inner chaos? Maybe we don't feel safe to talk about what we're feeling since we grew up in a home where we were told to "suck it up" and not express emotions. Perhaps we've suppressed or covered up our feelings for so long that we can't articulate our emotions beyond general overwhelm or frustration. We want to let go of what's got us in a tizzy and renew our minds with God's truth that brings calm. So why does emotional management feel like a superhuman feat some days? It's no wonder that we often stuff our authentic feelings behind a plastic smile and a cheery response of "yep, things are good!" Some days—or weeks and months—emotions feel like too much to handle.

I'm guessing you picked up this book because you're looking for practical tips to manage your emotions beyond simple platitudes like "pray harder" or "give it to God." While statements like these are true, let's be honest: when we're emotionally frustrated, Christian rhetoric can hurt more than help, even if it's well intended.

We all need easy-to-apply principles to determine a calm, Christ-centered response when the kids are driving us up a wall and our manager is acting like a jerk—again. When life hands us horrific curveballs, like the cancer diagnosis Kate received, we need to know what to do with all the anger, disappointment, and what-if questions. If nothing else, we need help taking control of what comes out of our mouths in heated moments, don't we?

If you want to better understand your emotional self and discover what it means to authentically honor your feelings in light of scriptural truth, then I'm glad you're here. That's exactly what we're going to talk about.

Starting right now, you and I have permission to relate to our emotions in a fresh new way. Here are four truths to get us started:

1. We don't have to run *from* our emotions or be driven *by* them. We are in control of how we respond.
2. We don't have to live in fear that giving our emotions a seat at the proverbial table will cause us to dismiss the authority of biblical truth. We can hold both emotions and truth at the same time.
3. We don't have to be imprisoned by the shame of how we've allowed out-of-control emotions to affect our relationships and self-esteem. We can step into the light of God's forgiveness and begin anew.
4. Not only can we reframe our relationship with our emotions but our emotions can be a unique, beautiful opportunity to reframe our relationship with Christ. God can use our up-and-down emotions to teach us about His character, grow us in holiness, and shower us with His love.

God walks beside us in every season, even when we're lost in emotional turmoil. He offers us compassion for our emotional ups and downs, helps us clarify what we're feeling inside, and equips us with courage to determine how to respond to our feelings in light of truth. Isn't that good news for stressed-out, emotionally overwhelmed people like you and me who are ready to discover what it means to manage emotions with confidence?

Why Is Managing Emotions So Hard?

Before we get too far along here, let's talk about the elephant in the room. Many of us see the damage of hiding, stuffing, or running from our emotions. So why do we stay stuck in our old patterns? Here are some big reasons why we avoid managing our emotions:

- We aren't equipped with tools to process our emotions well.
- We feel like we've tried to manage emotions in the past but haven't been successful.
- We view managing emotions as a painful, difficult process.
- We've convinced ourselves we're too busy and don't have time to manage emotions.
- We don't believe we're worth the energy and investment required to look at what's going on inside.
- We're afraid we'll uncover even more frustrating emotions or difficult truths about ourselves.
- We're afraid of how processing our emotions will negatively affect our relationships.
- We're afraid to discover what our emotions say about our relationship with God.

Which of these ring true for you? What other reasons might you add to the list? Take a moment to pause and consider what you tell yourself about why managing emotions is difficult.

To explore these statements further and to better understand why you struggle in managing emotions, download the free assessment from the link at the end of the chapter.

No matter which of these reasons resonates with you, I want you to know that I understand, because I've felt all of them. In fact, I spent most of my life being overwhelmed by my feelings and running from my emotions. That all changed in 2017 when years of pushing down the hurt caught up with me and nearly cost me my life.

My Story: How Unprocessed Emotions Almost Took My Life

The medical staff had finished their rounds for the night, and I was alone in the quiet, sterile atmosphere of the neurological intensive care unit. My thoughts were filled with the scary words the doctors shared a few hours before: "You had a vertebral artery dissection, and you're lucky to be alive."

I knew God was with me in that hospital room, but with the eerie rhythm of beeping machines in my ears and the drip-drip-drip of the blood thinner in my veins, I felt like a condemned criminal waiting for her executioner.

What would God say to me about the mess I'd made of my life?

Up to that point I would have said this forty-two-year-old mom of four young kids had a pretty good handle on things.

Yes, I stayed up too late—sleeping only four hours a night for twelve years straight.

Yes, I had a child with special needs and had taken on the bulk of his care (and that of his three younger siblings) since we had no family nearby to help.

Yes, I homeschooled my four kids while working full-time from home.

Yes, my husband had been out of work for over a year, and we'd been scraping the bottom of the barrel to feed our kids while considering a move out of state in order to survive financially.

And yes, I'd heard repeated warnings from well-intentioned family and friends: "Alicia, you really need to take better care of yourself or your body is going to give out on you."

I'd been suppressing all kinds of emotions in regard to these issues for a long time. But as an exhausted mom trying to hold it together for her family, I felt like I had neither the time, the skills, nor the luxury to address any of them. There was always a task to complete and someone who needed my help.

Along with ongoing money fears, continual work demands, and daily parenting frustrations, other deeply entrenched mental patterns silenced my emotions. Despite knowing who I was in Christ, perfectionism, performance, and people-pleasing were how I defined my worth. For as long as I could remember, a relentless inner taskmaster kept me tied to a hamster wheel of productivity. Now I see how these toxic mindsets were both my identity *and* my escape from my chaotic, overwhelming feelings.

I'd wanted to slow down, of course. I hated living so stressed-out all the time. I didn't want to be short with my kids and always lost in an anxious, worried spiral about, well . . . everything. But I had no clue *where* to start or *what* to do. So I did what I knew: I just kept going.

Until I couldn't. Until I found myself flat on my back in a hospital ICU room with an unexpected, life-threatening condition that left me unable to take care of myself or anyone else.

Until I found myself sitting alone in the quiet without any buffer between me, my emotions, and God.

The doctors had no medical explanation for why the arterial dissections took place, but in my heart, I *knew*. I knew that my poor self-care choices and ongoing emotional stress had finally caused my body to break down, and in the quiet, I heard God confirm those suspicions.[2]

I was concerned about the physical damage I'd done to myself, but frankly, I was more terrified about how to address the underlying issues that had gotten me there in the first place.

I knew that I needed more than just self-care hacks. I needed to determine and address the emotions behind the toxic behaviors that got me there. That meant finally facing some deep-rooted pain and heart-wrenching truths, which would perhaps be more excruciating than my physical recovery.

How Are We Managing (or Avoiding) Emotions?

I don't share my story for dramatic intrigue but to make a statement. I understand how paralyzing it can feel to even think about working through complicated, devastating emotions.

I also want to shout from the rooftops that running from what's inside will eventually catch up to us. We cannot outrun or hide away from the emotional effects of both the highly traumatic events and everyday drama of our lives. We must learn how to confidently work through our emotions with compassion for ourselves, clarity from God's Word, and courage to respond in a Christ-honoring manner.

Our brain is designed to keep us in a perceived state of safety by keeping things familiar, and this plays well with our desire to avoid uncomfortable feelings.[3] However, the reality is that even if we don't all end up flat on our back for nine months recovering from a life-threatening injury like I did, our mind, our physical body, and our soul are suffering *right now* if we're not managing negative emotions well.[4] We must learn how to lovingly address all those feelings swirling inside before they cause irreparable damage to our health and relationships.

Managing emotions is a skill that's neither taught nor modeled well in Western culture. I've seen that to be true for the thousands of Christian women I've interacted with as a conference speaker and through the personal stories I hear from the hundreds of godly women from my coaching practice. That's why it's not surprising that a recent survey of 115 of my female readers and podcast listeners who struggle with processing their feelings revealed that so many Christian women are ignoring and pushing down their emotions. Let's consider three questions women tend to ask in order to cope as well as the effect unprocessed emotions have on our relationships, our health, our confidence, and our spiritual well-being.

1. Prayer helps to release emotions, but do we pray for the wrong reasons?

Taking our troubles directly to God through prayer is one way that many of us were taught to handle our emotions. In fact, when asked to choose from a list of options on how they typically managed emotions, over 70 percent of survey respondents chose "I pray to ask God for help when dealing with difficult emotions." Since I surveyed a faith-based audience, it makes sense that this was the number one option women chose.

However, it's interesting to recognize that while nearly three-quarters of the group used prayer to cope with emotions—including 41 percent who said they "read or recite a Bible verse" to manage hard feelings—all the respondents shared their overall frustration about their inability to manage their emotions to the extent they desired. In other words, these women still struggle with emotional confidence even though they are seeking God for help with emotional management.

Maybe it sounds sacrilegious to even insinuate that God doesn't satisfy our emotional needs when the Bible shares that God is our comforter, peace, and safe refuge. No one is challenging that biblical truth, but let's consider what may be happening here.

When it comes to managing emotions, some seek God as a fix-it genie who's supposed to stop the pain and make it go away. Prayer can seem confusing when it feels like we've shared the emotions with God but have not seen any resolution to our problems.

Over and over in my clinical work I've seen that, for many, this cycle of praying without getting the desired outcome creates a break in relationship with God and makes it harder to trust Him in the future. This spiritual division can be so subtle that it may go unnoticed. Sometimes a person gives up praying altogether, but many times they keep up the ritual of prayer but lose hope that it's actually helping.

In addition, women often tell me that they know God's truth but can't believe it in their heart, even though they've actively participated in church and Bible study for years. They desire to know God, but this confusion or misunderstanding about how He's responded to them in past times of need can create a subconscious inner soundtrack that says "God is not trustworthy." The longer this pattern goes unchallenged and the more it is reinforced, the stronger this toxic inner dialogue becomes.

Naturally, prayer can bring comfort and direction when emotions run high. It's our essential lifeline to God and an integral aspect of ADD—the three-step emotional management tool we'll discuss in part 2. However, we must consider our posture and expectations when we pray through life's challenging emotions. I'd argue that it's not the lifeline itself (God) that's at fault here or even the communication method (prayer). Instead, it's the need for better tools to process and communicate what we're experiencing so that we are able to best receive God's direction for managing our emotions.

2. Staying busy can hide emotions, but at what cost?

The women I surveyed reported distraction as the second most popular emotional coping skill. When asked if they ignored painful emotions by staying busy in general, 44 percent said yes. In a separate question, nearly 59 percent said they use food, phone scrolling, alcohol, watching television, or shopping to comfort themselves when feeling unpleasant emotions.

I wonder how much heavier our emotions feel simply because they've had time to compound without being addressed. Like an infection, the longer we ignore the problem, the more painful it becomes. Plus, as the emotion festers, we find more reasons to be frustrated as new situations pop up that "confirm" the validity of what we're feeling. Staying busy to silence inner frustrations is partially effective in the moment, but what happens when life suddenly slows down and we lose access to the things that distract us?

This partially explains why anxiety and depression rates increased by 25 percent during the COVID-19 pandemic.[5] People no longer had overcrowded schedules to distract themselves from inner pain. At the same time, life became even more demanding as many took on extra responsibilities like increased childcare, homeschooling tasks, and, for some, extended work hours. Others lost loved ones or their jobs due to the economic downturn, which only added to the heartache and psychological stress.

The pandemic was the perfect storm to dismantle the "staying busy" fortress that many of us hide in to avoid navigating our feelings. Even though anxiety and depression levels have decreased since the height of the pandemic, we are still seeing the pandemic's aftereffects several years later, with anxiety and depression levels that are much higher than prepandemic levels.[6]

3. Staying positive temporarily boosts moods, but what about long-term shame when happiness eludes us?

When it comes to managing emotions, should we just stay positive? Gratitude journals and happiness mantras vote yes. I am a big believer in refocusing our thoughts from what author Joyce Meyer calls "stinkin'-thinkin'" to Scripture's life-giving truths.[7] Countless studies demonstrate gratitude's power to shift perspective, offer hope during dark times, and even improve physical health.[8] In fact, in my Christian Mindset Makeover course, I teach clients some of psychologist and author Dr. Rick Hanson's neuroscience principles on how we can "hardwire happiness" in the brain.

Gratitude and positivity, however, don't necessarily address the hurt underneath, and these wounds only compound the pain of difficult emotions. Despite being immersed in culture's messaging to "look on the bright side," many of the surveyed women shared how they felt like a failure because of their inability to deal with difficult feelings. We can't manage painful emotions by solely refocusing our thoughts on good ones. That's just more denial and dismissal.

Society's focus on staying positive sends a subtle-yet-toxic directive that's important to mention: good feelings need to be embraced, and painful feelings should be avoided. It's true that we're called to seek the joy of the Lord as our strength (Neh. 8:10), to rest in God's peace during all circumstances (Phil. 4:7), and to find comfort in His never-ending love (Lam. 3:22). And yes, we must take captive any thought or emotion that doesn't line up with God's promises (2 Cor. 10:5). These are essential aspects of staying emotionally and spiritually strong in Christ!

It's concerning, however, that we have hyperfocused on positive messaging and quietly slapped guilt and shame on our unpleasant emotions. Remember Kate Bowler and the overwhelming emotions she felt after finding out she had cancer? In her book *No Cure for Being Human*, Kate shares, "Everyone is now a televangelist of the gospel of good, better, best. But (the fact is) I cannot out-work or out-pace or out-pray my cancer. I can't dispel it with a can-do attitude."[9]

Some situations cannot be avoided, solved, or passed over, but instead must be passed *through*. If we believe that we must always stay positive, then it's easy to conclude that there must be something wrong with us or that we're not "good enough" Christians when we can't hold it all together. This is one of Satan's biggest lies.

Nearly 34 percent of survey respondents said, "I fear that my difficult emotions don't fit with the image of what a Christian woman should be." In addition, when asked how they handle unpleasant emotions, more than half (52 percent) admitted that they push their emotions down, try to stay positive, and hide their feelings from others while 34 percent said they push their feelings down and just tell themselves to believe truth. How much of this pressure to hide emotions is due to the ever-increasing pressure to keep up a "good Christian girl" front?

Covering up painful emotions with positive rhetoric is not the answer. Neither is demonizing emotions for their existence. In upcoming chapters, we will explore a healthy middle ground.

How Does Suppressed Emotion Affect Relationships and Contribute to the Loneliness Epidemic?

Many survey participants admitted that out-of-control emotions had caused all kinds of relationship drama and cited that they struggled with expressing themselves without appearing defensive. One woman said, "I don't know how to express myself without feelings of guilt or that it's all my fault." Twenty-seven percent of respondents shared that they quiet any emotion that feels "too disruptive in their relationship with God or others" because they are afraid it will "rock the boat."

How in the world are we supposed to experience emotional closeness and intimacy with loved ones when we can't express the frustration of unmet expectations or feel safe to share how others have wounded us?

Society is struggling with a loneliness epidemic, and emotional suppression further contributes to feelings of division and separation. A recent report from the US Surgeon General states that from 2003 to 2020 the amount of time Americans spent alone increased by twenty-four hours a month and social engagement with friends decreased by twenty hours a month.[10] Social isolation and relational emptiness only amplify that inner voice that says we're "odd," something is "wrong with us," and we're the "only one" who struggles like this.

Not only can learning to manage emotions improve relationships with others and aid social connection but the ability to regulate emotions well is associated with greater well-being, increased financial success, and higher socioeconomic status.[11] Truly, learning to manage our emotions can improve our lives in so many ways!

How Are Poorly Managed Emotions Affecting the Church?

Unprocessed emotions are also having a disastrous impact on our ability to trust God and grow in spiritual maturity. Many Christians are familiar with God's command to take their thoughts captive but aren't taught how to make this happen in the real world. As a result, they can't shake negative thought patterns and aren't equipped to manage difficult emotions. And as stated above, they feel enormous pressure to be continually joyful as part of their duty to represent Christ well to unbelievers.

If we're not equipped to deal with toxic thought patterns and are encouraged to always focus on godly joy during difficult times, we create an inner conflict between how we feel and what we know to be true about God. We may logically know that we are fully loved and worthy in Christ, but we have a hard time living in the reality of this biblical truth because unresolved difficult emotions have created an internal dialogue that we're still unloved, unworthy, and not enough.

This has also cultivated a "just stay positive" mindset that leaves many confused about God's love and His will. They ask, *Is God still good when life hurts? And if so, what do I do with my disappointments and pain in light of God's promises to bring blessing to His people?* One woman said it this way, "I'm frustrated by all the hard things happening in my life. Why are things so hard when God promises to give me an abundant life?"

There is an extra layer of shame when we feel pressured to always appear joyful in order to not "ruin our witness" for the gospel. Though we always want to represent Christ well, think about this—were joy and peace the only emotions that Christ exemplified? How do we deal with the fact that so many Bible heroes did not spend their days bouncing from one cloud of happiness to another? How do we handle books like Lamentations—not to mention a majority of the psalms—that express extreme heartache and pain?

Unprocessed emotions create opportunities for the enemy to slowly erode a Christian's faith as he whispers lies about God's character and trustworthiness. If these lies are not processed against biblical truth and discarded, these quiet murmurs build walls of mistrust with God and cause Christians to turn away from Him in times of trouble.

Unfortunately, this slow faith erosion is exactly what we see happening in our churches. As a result of these inner attacks on identity, many transition to an outward, works-based faith that's more about checking boxes than inner transformation. We keep up appearances but wonder why God seems far away. The result is dry, meaningless religion that transforms neither an individual nor a society and leaves many hiding their authentic selves behind a smiling, "everything is okay" mask.

How Does Being Emotionally Illiterate Add to Our Emotional Dysfunction?

In her book *Dare to Lead*, author Brené Brown states that the vast majority of people she interviewed are not comfortable in the language of emotions. "Emotional literacy is, in my opinion, as critical as having language," she says. "When we can't name and articulate what's happening to us we can't move through it." She compares this emotional illiteracy to going to a doctor with an excruciating pain and not being able to describe it because we have duct tape over our mouth and our hands are tied behind our back. The doctor wants to help, but because we can't describe what's going on, we can't find the healing we need.[12]

Imagine how much our relationships, self-esteem, and overall sanity would be improved if we learned to speak the language of emotions! With practical tools to understand and express them in healthy ways, we can experience ongoing mental rejuvenation that not only relieves stress but also allows us to know ourselves better and to use our emotions to grow in godliness. With emotional tools in hand, it would be so much easier to contextualize suffering, failure, and disappointment as natural parts of life and opportunities to grow and be strengthened in light of the gospel.

Are You Tired Enough of the Pain to Make a Change?

In order to enact change we must make it personal. Even if we can recognize when we're emotionally stuck, the ultimate question is what we will do with the information. Will we be willing to learn new skills and implement them?

Let me make this personal: Are you frustrated enough with how you currently manage emotions that you're willing to try something new?

If we want lasting change in any situation, we must be more uncomfortable staying where we are than we are with the discomfort of moving forward. Animals and even single-celled organisms are biologically wired to move *toward* pleasure and *away* from pain (a concept known as Thorndike's Law of Effect),[13] and that's ultimately true of human behavior as well. To make change, we must understand the pain we're moving from and the pleasure we're moving toward.

The first step in making change is to get a clear sense of your current situation. To determine how ignoring or hiding from underlying emotions is affecting you, your relationships, and your ability to show up healthy and whole, download the free exercise "How Are Out of Control Emotions Affecting Your Life?" at the link provided at the end of the chapter.

By the way, you don't need to know *how* the emotional change will happen yet. I'm asking you to trust me on that part. First let's work on *what's* happening and *why* it matters in this assessment. Deal?

When you're done with the assessment, join me in chapter 2 where we'll get started on the path to transformation by defining what emotions are, how the brain processes them, how they relate to core needs, and much more.

CHAPTER QUESTIONS

1. How would you rate your current ability to manage your emotions in a healthy way? Has that ability changed or remained the same as you've experienced different life seasons or issues?

2. Do you use coping mechanisms to hide from or to stuff your emotions? If so, which do you most commonly use?

3. Do you agree with the statement that Christian culture has affected our ability to vulnerably share about difficult emotions? Why or why not?

4. Do you feel pressured to act like you are always joyful and have it all together? If so, how has that affected your relationship with God?

5. Would you consider yourself emotionally literate? Why or why not?

Testimonial

I used to be depressed all the time and felt very hopeless. I saw people around me being happy and I didn't understand how to get there.

I finally got tired of living like that. I wanted something more, and that gave me the tiniest bit of courage to grow in understanding my feelings. These little decisions to lean into my emotions became little bright spots of hope and happiness as I saw my fog lifting. I realized that I didn't ever want to go back to that place, and that's my greatest motivation to stay emotionally connected with myself and others.

Brianna, coaching client

QUESTION

I'm tired of dealing with the same emotions over and over. How can I stop feeling emotionally defeated and have hope that I can have a different response?

ANSWER

I understand and sense the guilt, shame, and heaviness behind this question. It's hard when you want things to change but you're not sure how to make it happen or why the things you tried in the past didn't work. Here are some questions to process, possibly in a journal:

- If you were to look at your situation from the outside, what would you say are some of the triggers or biggest pain points?
- What's true about your situation, and what lies are you telling yourself?
- What's in your control to change? What's outside of your control and must be released to God?
- What parts of these challenging emotions do you need to confess as sin, apologize to others, or take responsibility for in some other way?

These are big questions and it's okay to take your time as you think through them. Start that conversation about these questions with God now and then keep a journal handy to write down any insights you hear from Him.

Don't forget to check out the free downloads for *Emotional Confidence*! There's a quiz, helpful exercises, and even audio and video tools to help you continue your journey in managing your emotions.

Go to AliciaMichelle.com/Emotional-Downloads to access these free resources.

2

Understanding and Defining Emotions

Now that we've seen the devastating impact that out-of-control emotions can have on our relationships with others, with ourselves, and with God, how can we break free from emotional chaos and gather a fresh perspective on managing our feelings?

In this chapter we will lay the groundwork for better emotional management as well as the ADD method by considering what emotions are and how they develop in the brain, how feelings relate to core needs, and what mental filters and biological processes affect how we process emotional triggers. While I am going to use some fancy terms from brain science and psychology, my goal is to equip you with core knowledge on the topic and not to overwhelm you with jargon. Grab your favorite hot beverage and let's dive into the wonderful and wacky world of human emotions.

What Are Emotions?

First, let's define emotions and feelings. The American Psychological Association describes *emotion* as a "complex reaction pattern, involving experiential, behavioral and physiological elements, by which an individual attempts to deal with a personally significant matter or event."[1] Scientists state that *emotions* are the result of an unconscious evaluation of a situation while *feelings* are a conscious reflection of that unconscious assessment.[2] For our purposes, we'll keep it simple and use the terms interchangeably.

From a spiritual perspective, emotions are a natural part of how we're wired to react to all that we experience. God created emotions as sensory tools to help us understand and respond to our world, just like He created our nerve endings to help us experience the sensation of touch and our taste buds to enjoy the flavor of food. Emotions like happiness, pleasure, and peace are often the first signs that all is well—or, as in the case of emotions like outrage, sadness, and shame, that all is *not* well—in our relationship with ourselves, with God, and with the world.

Ever seen the check engine light in your car? We can think of emotions as God's check engine light on our soul. Emotions alert us that our soul is off-balance, just like the check engine light tells us when our car needs service.

Emotions are neither bad nor good but serve as neutral indicators of what's happening inside. Do we get mad at our car because the check engine light comes on? It's never fun to see that light, but at the end of the day we're appreciative for the alert because it tells us something's not right. From this perspective, we can see painful emotions as compassionate invitations to slow down and ask ourselves what's going on. Emotions should be viewed not as an enemy to fight but a curiosity to consider.

They are a normal part of how God designed humans to respond to the world, but like all things in creation, emotions must be filtered through the authoritative lens of God's truth. Our emotions can identify a distorted view of the truth because they are created by our flawed human minds and are affected by our genetics, experiences, and cultural upbringing. We can honor emotions as an honest reflection of what we're experiencing, yet Scripture must be our ultimate guiding light.

How Do We Experience Emotions?

While all humans share basic emotions that are innate and universal, each of us expresses those emotions uniquely. And that emotional expression varies based on how emotions interact with an individual's personality, family background, genetic encoding, and more. Some of us are neurologically wired as *highly sensitive people* and have the potential to sense, experience, and express emotions more than others.[3]

Does it feel like your emotions are stacked on top of each other? Emotions are often layered to create various combinations of perception. We can experience two or more sometimes-opposing emotions at once. For example, we've all felt *nerve-cited*, a colloquialism expressing feeling both nervous and excited at once, or *bittersweet*, feeling both happy and sad about a circumstance.

Emotions can build over time as repeated triggers and experiences are reinforced in the brain to create emotional stimulus-response patterns that affect behavior. For instance, let's say it was regularly modeled to us as a child that it was wrong to make mistakes. Because of this imprinting, our brain may feel shame in response to any imperfections (emotional pattern), and as a result we find emotional safety in surface-level relationships in order to hide our flaws from others. Unless the pattern is interrupted, we continue to strengthen this emotional response to the trigger.[4]

Experiencing emotions, especially intense emotions, often involves our physical, intellectual, and spiritual selves.[5] A fascinating study by a team of Finnish biomedical engineers demonstrated how emotions can manifest in our physical bodies, noting that emotions like love, pride, anger, and happiness showed activation in areas like the head, arms, and chest, while emotions like sadness and depression signaled a decrease in body sensation to areas like the head, arms, and legs.[6] Our physical bodies react to our emotions, which is why we'll cover emotional management tools that intentionally involve our entire body in later chapters.

Ever felt like you could not shake a particular emotion or wondered why it feels like some emotions tend to linger longer than others? Studies show that the intensity or quantity of emotions attached to a situation increases the likelihood that the memory will imprint on our brain.[7] This is one reason why we can often vividly remember intensely pleasurable or highly painful incidents. In addition, studies show that some emotions do last longer than others. A Belgian study shared that sadness was the longest-lasting emotion, while others like surprise, boredom, relief, and disgust were the shortest.[8]

Interestingly, researchers have also found that male and female brains respond to emotions differently. A Harvard Medical School study found that females have larger volumes in both their frontal cortices (the learning, thinking, and judging brain centers) and limbic cortices (the emotional processing center) and that some of these differences explain why women tend to be more emotional and to worry more than men.[9] Other neuroscience studies suggest that women tend to use more emotional-focused coping strategies, like rumination, to deal with their feelings while men used more cognitive coping strategies, like detachment and rationalization, to manage reactions.[10]

What's our takeaway here? While we do have much control over how we handle our feelings, it's helpful to understand some of the psychological and biological components at play so we can navigate our feelings with compassion and grace.

Two Categories of Emotions

Now that we've identified some of the hidden components of how emotions form and are strengthened, how can we begin to classify what we're feeling? Psychologists often separate emotions into two groups: *basic* and *complex*. Let's take a quick look at each.

Basic emotions, sometimes called *simple emotions*, are instinctual, hardwired responses to our world.[11] Theories abound on which emotions should be classified as basic, but emotional psychologist Paul Ekman originally placed sadness, happiness, fear, anger, surprise, and disgust in this category.[12]

On the other hand, *complex emotions* utilize an infinite combination of basic emotions and are affected by past experience and logical reasoning. For example, the complex emotion of hate can be a fusion of anger, fear, and disgust, but the exact expression of hate varies by individual since each person has unique interpretations based on their experiences and learned behavior.[13]

In 1982 psychotherapist Gloria Wilcox created the *feelings wheel* (see the figure below).[14]

Arranged in a similar concentric format as a color wheel, the feelings wheel demonstrates how emotions can blend together to create new feelings and build the nuances of a specific emotion. The colors of the feelings wheel intensify in coordination with how intense the emotional expression is of that particular feeling. Like a traditional color wheel, opposite sides of a feelings wheel reflect opposing emotions. Many find the feelings wheel helpful when trying to expand an emotional feeling beyond a basic feeling, like "I am mad" to something more descriptive like "I am skeptical."

While variations of feelings wheels differ based on which emotions are included, these helpful tools typically include basic emo-

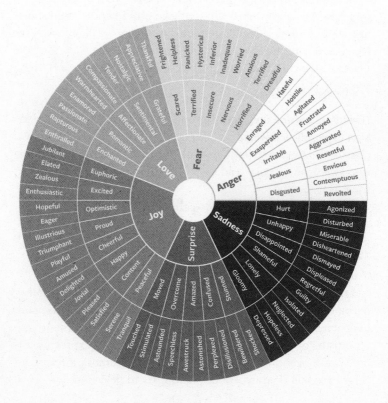

tions like *fear*, *anger*, *sadness*, *surprise*, *joy*, and *love* in the middle, with less intense variants of the emotion radiating from the center. Notice, for example, how the basic emotion *joy* can be broken down into more specific emotions like *euphoric* or *excited*. These two emotions can be translated even further to become *jubilant*, *elated*, *zealous*, or *enthusiastic*.

The Brain Uses Thoughts, Emotions, and Experiences to Create Beliefs

So how do our thoughts play a role in our emotional response? While our thoughts make assessments about a specific situation, our emotions indicate *how* we interpret those assessments in relationship to ourselves or others. For instance, if we *think* "I am not enough," we *feel* shame or sadness as we interpret how the thought of not being enough affects our ability to be the person we long to be. Or if we receive news of rejection, we may first think something like "that turned out differently than what I expected." Depending on other mental or biological components at play, our emotional response to the rejection could include disappointment, mistrust, anger, or even acceptance.

As we encounter both heartache and happiness in this world, our mind continually processes our thoughts by using filters like past experience to create our unique emotional response. Suppose that we listen to a specific song on the radio. Hearing that song may evoke feelings of sadness for you because it reminds you of a painful relationship breakup, but perhaps for me it brings joy because I have a memory of playing that song on my family's annual road trip to the beach.

How do repeated thoughts affect our beliefs and therefore our emotions? Scientists share that when a thought combines with an emotion and is replayed over and over, a belief is formed.[15] Because many of these emotional beliefs are formed on a subconscious level—as the brain interprets stimuli and determines how to make sense of the data it receives from the outside world—a belief can quickly cement into what feels like fact as it is reinforced through repetition. These beliefs may or may not be true according to God's Word. We must pay attention to our beliefs, especially those around how we define our identity, because the brain makes decisions, takes action, and produces results based on these internal beliefs.

In addition, brain science demonstrates that thoughts and emotions are strengthened when they are repeated regularly. *Neuroplasticity* means that our neurological connections—how we see and interpret the world—are continually being shaped by our thoughts and experiences.[16] Our brains are different today from how they were six months ago based on what we've seen, felt, and mentally reinforced in this time period.[17] Repeated thoughts and emotions can easily become patterned belief systems that either help or harm us. This is why it's understandable that God encourages us to "take captive every thought" (2 Cor. 10:5) and to "guard our heart" (Prov. 4:23). The mental habits we create today build the future mind we have tomorrow.

The great news? No matter the state of our emotional patterning now, there is always room for healing.

One final encouraging thought on this topic: scientists have discovered that we're given around 1,400 new neurons to respond to our world every day.[18] Each of these neurons is ready to receive new programming and new perspectives. I consider them 1,400 daily chances to rethink how we think. Isn't this a beautiful, tangible representation of God's promise to give us new mercies every morning (Lam. 3:22–23)?

How Do Emotions Relate to Core Needs?

You've probably heard of the concept of *core needs*—those essential human desires we're given that underlie our behavior. Emotions can be positive or negative indicators, those "check engine lights," to use our previous metaphor of how well our core needs are being met.

There are many ways scientists have classified core needs, but psychologist Abraham Maslow's hierarchy of needs is perhaps the most commonly cited. Maslow theorized that our needs are stacked in a pyramid format, starting at the bottom with physiological needs (water, food, shelter), then moving upward to safety needs (personal security, health, employment), love and belonging (friendship, family, connection), esteem (recognition, self-worth, uniqueness), and finally self-actualization (creativity, purpose, morality).[19]

How might this plethora of needs manifest in everyday emotional struggles? *Schema therapy* theorizes that psychological problems we face as adults originate in our core emotional childhood needs not being satisfied in healthy ways.[20] In my experience, behaviors like perfectionism, performance, and people-pleasing can often be traced back to what we learned about confidence, social acceptance, and self-worth at an early age. In addition, psychotherapist Klaus Grawe defined four psychological needs—the need for attachment, the need for control, the need for pleasure and avoidance of pain, and the need for self-enhancement. He theorized that humans are driven to satisfy these needs either in healthy or unhealthy ways. In many coaching interactions, I see how several of these needs—especially the need for control—are the root of a client's conflict around feeling safe to move through fear and trust God.

Personality typing systems like the Enneagram offer explanations for how associated fears and desires drive emotion and behavior. Someone who classifies as a Two on the Enneagram, for example, has a fear of being unwanted or unloved by others,[21] and these emotional needs can lead to healthy behaviors like establishing emotional boundaries when serving and caring for others, or unhealthy behaviors like people-pleasing in order to meet a Two's need to be appreciated and valued. I appreciate when my coaching clients share their results from these types of self-assessment tools because it helps clarify their core motivations and offers direction for how to heal from painful emotions and unhealthy thought patterns.

Ultimately, we must remember that hunger for purpose and meaning are core needs that only God can meet. God created a hunger inside us to know Him and to be in ongoing, honest communion with Him. Scripture shows how all our physical, emotional, and spiritual needs are met through a relationship with Christ. If that connection is blocked or hindered in any way, we can be left searching for wholeness and happiness in all the wrong places.

Most of the Christian women I work with struggle with a collection of toxic beliefs about their relationship with God or about God Himself. These inner thought patterns are a collection of half-truths cultivated from unmet expectations, past hurts, present frustrations, and fears of the future that dramatically shape how they currently view God or how they perceive God views them. Some have covered up these faith dichotomies and "why" questions for so long with years of "good Christian girl" behavior that it's a bit of a surprise when they're revealed. Many haven't made the connection between how their deep emotional frustrations are linked to unresolved issues with God around core needs for trust and safety. It's beautiful to watch these women step into unbridled confidence and joy once we gently and compassionately address the root of these lies!

Common Mental Filters That Affect Emotional Processing

Much like camera filters alter the reality of a photograph, mental filters can radically transform how we process emotions. Powerful feelings like anger and grief can cloud our vision, causing us to lean into assumptions or half-truths. It's common to get stuck in negative emotional patterns, especially when dealing with the same emotional triggers over and over and not seeing difficult situations resolve.

Speaking of negativity, why do so many of us struggle with negative thoughts in general? Neuroscience shows that our brains tend to focus on the negative instead of the positive, a term called *negativity bias*, so that our brain can be more attentive to potential threats.[22] Psychologist Dr. Rick Hanson explains negativity bias as "the mind being like Velcro for negative experiences and Teflon for positive ones." Whether because of nature or nurture, some of us have a stronger negativity bias than others, and naturally this affects how we process emotions.[23]

While negativity bias can keep us aware of harm, it's easy to see how this mental filter can make it harder to dwell on God's promises and future hope, especially during life's challenges. Like any mental filter, it's critical that we ask ourselves questions like, Am I looking at this clearly? and How does Scripture see this issue? Like an architect uses a blueprint for building construction, we need the plumb line of biblical facts and the leading of the Holy Spirit to help us process emotions.

Shame and fear can also greatly affect our ability to process emotions in a healthy way. Likewise, if we live with the bondage of guilt and shame, it can be so tempting to self-protect by living small and shrinking our presence to others. There are so many ways that unhealthy thought patterns, whether subconscious or conscious, can make us our own worst enemies in terms of processing emotions. If there's trauma and unprocessed pain in your life, I recommend working with a Christian mental health professional to find healing.

And as we find healing for the root causes behind emotional patterns, there will be less out-of-control, in-the-moment emotional spillover to manage in our relationships. Susan, one of my coaching clients, told me about an aha moment when she realized she wasn't really angry about her family's tiny infractions, such as her husband forgetting to close the garage door, but that the real cause of her anger was feeling unappreciated by her family members. That low-level, ongoing frustration about feeling unnoticed and taken for granted had developed a bitterness inside her that spilled out regularly on her loved ones. Once she resolved this deeper emotional tension, interactions with her family became much more pleasant.

Our ability to clearly process emotions can also be affected by other mental health diagnoses, such as anxiety or depression or physical disorders that can lead to mental health conditions. And let's not forget how fluctuating hormones can toss a flaming torch into an already kindled firestorm of feelings.

If we're working through difficult feelings attached to complicated issues, like a strained relationship or a long-term life trial, we're quicker to attach words like *always* and *never* to our emotional responses. This black-or-white thinking can not only greatly skew our ability to gain an accurate perception of our circumstances but it can keep us emotionally stuck in negative thought patterns.

I struggled with black-or-white thinking after walking with my husband through eighteen months of unemployment in 2017. Fear and pain had trapped us in survival mode, and as a result, it was much easier to assume the worst and keep negative thoughts on repeat. It would have been so easy to let thoughts like "things will always be this way" wash over me. But as I noticed how disappointment and hopelessness were attempting to lock me into despair, I chose to actively fight to dwell in contentment and trust each day.

Mental filters don't always have to be negative. We can also use positive filters to change how we interact with our emotions. "What if it's easy?" is one of my favorite positive mental filters, especially when someone feels defeated and overwhelmed by emotional processing. This phrase is not meant to be a flippant or naive perspective that negates difficult feelings or real struggles. Instead, "what if it's easy?" is a mental decision to focus on God's partnership with us in every situation. Any task we do with God lowers our stress because when we recognize our limits and release what's out of our control, Jesus promises that our burden will be lighter (Matt. 11:30).

Will we pay attention to any mental filters that may be present as we process emotions? Will we choose to ask God, "What's the truth about how I'm processing these feelings?" Because how we *perceive* our emotions greatly affects how we *respond* to them.

Are You a Fighter, Runner, Freezer, or Pleaser?

No discussion of emotional perception and response would be complete without talking about a very important brain structure known as the *amygdala*. While brain imaging scans show that emotions arise from various networks in the brain,[24] the amygdala's fight-or-flight response is often behind many of our emotional responses.

If our brain's ultimate job is to keep us safe, then the amygdala's job is to alert us to any threats to that safety. The amygdala's two almond-shaped structures detect threats on a conscious and unconscious level and regulate behavioral and physiological responses to those threats as part of our brain's limbic system. It also contributes to both long-term and in-the-moment decision-making using instinctive and learned behavioral responses to respond to environmental triggers.[25]

How does the fight-or-flight response work? Think of the amygdala as a highly trained soldier that's continually scanning the horizon for threats from their station on the roof of a building. When the amygdala notices something potentially dangerous, it kicks off a chain of complex biochemical reactions involving internal systems, including the sympathetic nervous system, in order to respond quickly to the threat, such as to increase the level of the hormone cortisol.[26] Our body responds to this chemical change with an increased heart rate, faster and shallower breathing, and more blood flow to our extremities so our muscles are prepared for defense. Fear, anger, anxiety, and aggression flood our minds as part of this response.

The fight-or-flight response is incredibly helpful when we're in a true life-or-death situation, but all too often in our modern world, the amygdala's reaction can be an overreaction. Psychologist Daniel Goleman coined the term *amygdala hijack* to describe when the response to stress rises above logical thinking.[27]

It's important to note that when we're stuck in an amygdala hijack, our logical brain is not in control. This is why we can find ourselves doing irrational things to bring pleasure and avoid pain, such as locking ourselves in the pantry and voraciously devouring a bag of chocolate chip cookies. It's only when the moment passes and the logical brain comes back online that we take stock of what's happened. If the amygdala hijacking resulted in a poor choice, that's when the guilt and self-loathing settle in.

Fight, *flight*, *freeze*, and *please* are four patterns that describe how the amygdala's instinctual response processes emotions.[28] *Fight* is an aggressive response to the threat, such as using confrontation to emotionally defend ourselves. *Flight* is a desire to run from the conflict, such as hiding from or avoiding the threat. *Freeze* is our body's inability to move, which may look like overanalyzing and ruminating on our feelings. *Please* (sometimes referred to as *fawn*) is an unhealthy desire to make others happy since it often looks like silencing our own feelings in order to avoid conflict.[29] Sometimes we can use a combination of these responses to convey our true emotions, such as passive-aggressive behavior that uses both the fight and please responses.

Remember how the brain loves repetition? Like any trigger-response behavior, over time the brain reinforces fight-or-flight response patterns based on how often they are repeated. Yes, it's a bit frustrating that these amygdala responses can become even more automatic based on our own conditioning! Using the fight, flight, freeze, or please model, I think of each of these conditioned responses to managing our feelings as different personas:

As a *fighter*, we use harsh language to judge our thoughts and emotions;

as a *runner*, we use distraction to numb and hide from our thoughts and emotions;

as a *freezer*, we use overthinking to nullify our ability to take action on our thoughts and emotions; and

as a *pleaser*, we use dismissal to squelch any thoughts or emotions that could cause conflict with others.

These fight, run, freeze, please personas make sense as self-defense mechanisms. If we don't have the emotional skills to lovingly acknowledge and address these patterns regularly, then it's understandable why so many of us stay stuck in them. Without intentional noticing and practical tools, we can easily *react* to triggers instead of thoughtfully *responding* to them.

Thankfully, there's hope. Not only can these behavioral and neurological patterns be reversed but God gave us the spiritual fruit of self-control to override our biological conditioning and the Holy Spirit to bring truth to the forefront when we're tempted to participate in sinful behavioral patterns (1 Cor. 10:13). Our past does not have to dictate our future. We don't have to let our conditioned responses take over and override truth! More on that soon, I promise.

For now, you're invited to notice some of your own fight-or-flight triggers and behavioral patterns. You can also download the free quiz "Are You a Fighter, Runner, Freezer, or Pleaser?" from the link at the end of the chapter to learn more about your amygdala-driven responses to stress.

CHAPTER QUESTIONS

1. Which of these truths about emotions was most insightful for you?
2. Do you have any core emotional needs that are not being met? If so, what are they?
3. What are some mental filters that affect how you process your feelings?
4. What are some everyday triggers that cause you to experience out-of-control or uncomfortable emotions?

Testimonial

I looked back at a journal from a year ago, and it was really encouraging to see how my thoughts and feelings have evolved after using ADD. I used to be a slave to my emotions, especially my anger. My inner voice was so accusatory and self-hating. Now I'm much more able to separate myself from my emotions and release control to God. I am way more compassionate to myself and to others now. It is really encouraging to see how my inner dialogue has changed and my relationship with God has grown! A huge weight has finally lifted from my shoulders—one that's been there for ten to fifteen years.

Rebecca, coaching client

QUESTION

How do hurt and trauma affect how we experience emotions?

ANSWER

While I am not a trauma-informed mental health professional, I can attest to the effect of trauma in my life and in my family members' and clients' lives. Since the brain is designed to respond to its environment, it makes perfect sense that hurt and trauma can negatively affect healthy emotional processing. Let's look at this more closely by considering the fact that our brain is wired to keep us safe. However, there are moments when we cannot flee a traumatic situation and we are forced to stay in the painful circumstances. Trauma splits us off from a healthy primal response, and if the brain is not able to process and release the emotion in a healthy way, it responds by shutting down emotionally or stuffing the feelings.

Seeing others model unhealthy behavior or enduring a traumatic experience can strengthen future unhealthy mental patterns. For example, Oprah Winfrey shared her story of how childhood trauma turned her into a pleaser and that has made it hard for her to navigate her emotions. "When you've been groomed to be compliant . . . you were taught you can't say no," she shared. "The sense that you are deserving enough to set your own boundaries has been stolen from you. For years I would say yes to things I knew I didn't want to do or avoid difficult conversations because I could not live with the discomfort of speaking up for myself."[30]

Trauma's influence on our emotions is a huge topic. For further explanation, I recommend books like *The Body Keeps the Score* by Bessel van der Kolk.

Don't forget to check out the free downloads for *Emotional Confidence*! There's a quiz, helpful exercises, and even audio and video tools to help you continue your journey in managing your emotions.

Go to AliciaMichelle.com/Emotional-Downloads to access these free resources.

3

6 Truths about Emotions to Better Interpret All the Feels

There's nothing like a good emotional freak-out to make us feel like we've blown our Christian witness. A friend recently told me, "I have an idea in my head of the kind of woman of God I'm supposed to be. But when I experience emotions that are the opposite of that image, it's embarrassing and frustrating."

Yep. We've all been there. We try our hardest to be kind and grace-filled women who represent Christ well, but despite our best intentions, we've all had those moments when our accumulated feelings burst through the surface and our I've-got-it-all-together facade crumbles into an angry, and often displaced, torrent of "why is it so hard to figure out where the large stainless-steel pot goes in the cabinet?!"

And then there are those moments when our emotions catch us off guard. You know, when we find ourselves yelling, "What in the world? NOOO!!!" as our eight-year-old smears his orange Cheeto-fingers all over the white couch.

Managing challenging emotions can feel like having an out-of-body experience where you know what to do but can't seem to make it happen. We wonder, *What's wrong with me? Why can't*

I just keep it together? Maybe we understand *what* caused the frustration but hate that we let our feelings manifest into hurtful words and actions. Guilt and shame settle in as we, once again, condemn ourselves for missing the mark.

Like I've said before, I'm not here to justify emotions that lead to sinful actions. When we make mistakes, we must own up to them, confess any sin, and apologize to anyone we hurt. We don't need to heap shame on ourselves when our emotions get the best of us. By God's grace, we can learn from our mistakes and move on in freedom.

But wouldn't it be nice to avoid the emotional freak-out in the first place?

In this chapter we'll get one step closer to better managing— and even avoiding—those emotional freak-outs by understanding six truths about our feelings. These six truths can help us find new clarity and freedom when it comes to processing challenging emotions. They are the building blocks we'll use for better applying the ADD emotional management tool that we'll explore in future chapters.

These truths will help us focus our perspective on the One who invented the idea of emotions, and who, thankfully, wants to partner with us in managing them.

Truth #1: God Designed Us as Emotional Creatures

As humans we are uniquely created in God's image, and this means that we share some of His characteristics, including the ability to experience emotions.

God the Father demonstrates a wide range of emotions, and from the first pages of Scripture we learn that He is an emotional being who responds to His creation. In each day of the creation narrative, God the Father steps back from His work to enjoy what He has formed by proclaiming it "good." The Bible notes how He can feel anger, regret, sorrow, compassion, mercy, love, and kindness.[1] We can assume He is familiar with every emotion since He is the creator of all things, and He promises to walk with us through every circumstance (Ps. 104:24). He repeatedly states key emotional characteristics, such as being "slow to anger" and "abounding in love and faithfulness," as essential parts of His identity (Exod. 34:6).

The other members of the Trinity display emotions as well. The Holy Spirit can experience grief and joy and fills our hearts with His love, hope, tenderness, and compassion.[2] In the Bible we see that Jesus was angry about the Pharisees' hypocritical, judgmental nature, filled with sadness when His friend Lazarus died, and endured such great anxiety and sorrow that He sweat blood in the garden of Gethsemane.[3]

The Bible recognizes that emotions like weeping, laughing, and celebrating are a normal part of life (Eccles. 3:4). We are told to share in others' emotions by rejoicing with those who rejoice and mourning with those who mourn as part of our call to carry each other's burdens and fulfill the law of Christ (Rom. 12:15; Gal. 6:2). Even Song of Solomon poetically recounts and celebrates the fierce emotional bond between two lovers.

If God exhibits emotions and designed us in His image, then we can view our feelings as beautiful, God-designed mechanisms for interaction and response—a sixth sense of sorts. We can respect and honor our emotions as they come. Though we may share God's ability to display emotion, our feelings are processed through imperfect human bodies, so they are not necessarily divine expressions. Our emotions are still subject to the authority of God's Word.

Truth #2: God Wants to Meet Our Unique Emotional Needs

Along with the ability to express emotions, God has wired us to have certain core emotional needs met, several of which we mentioned in chapter 2. God acknowledges the human need to belong, to be loved, and to be acknowledged in Mark 1:11 when He proclaims to Jesus at His baptism, "You are my Son, whom I love; with you I am well pleased." Likewise, we can argue that God the Father meets Jesus's human need for purpose and worth when He exclaims, "This is my Son. . . . Listen to him!" at the Transfiguration (Matt. 17:5).

God the Father can also meet our specific needs, such as how He satisfied Adam's emotional need for companionship by creating a custom-made partner (Gen. 2:18, 21–23); how He comforted Leah by allowing her to conceive after noticing that she was not loved by her husband (29:31); and how He healed Naomi's bitterness by giving her a faithful, loving daughter-in-law (Ruth 1:16).

While all our needs are fully met in our relationship with Christ, God can use other people to meet our emotional needs in unique ways. Aaron helped Moses in his insecurity about his ability to speak well before the Israelite people (Exod. 4:14–16); Jonathan risked his life to befriend David and served as a buffer between David and Saul's fighting (1 Sam. 19:1–5); Jesus deepened the connection between John the disciple and Jesus's mother Mary while both stood watching Jesus's crucifixion (John 19:25–27).

God challenges us to use our trials as opportunities to comfort others (2 Cor. 1:3–4). While we may not be emotionally close with every person we meet, even an unexpected kindness from a coffee-house barista can remind us of God's loving presence. If you're an animal lover like me, you know how our beloved pets can be models of godly companionship, trust, and utter joy. My four dogs follow me everywhere, and they bring me untold laughter, love, and comic relief, which are essential elements of emotional health.

We may live in an ever-darkening world, but God's presence fills every corner of it. He's committed to helping us manage our up-and-down responses to this broken reality. He sees us in our distress, and we can trust Him to provide for all that we emotionally experience.

Truth #3: God Welcomes Our Emotional Messiness and Wants to Help Us Manage Our Emotions

Crying is one of the most dramatic physical manifestations of our emotions, and the Bible is full of stories of weeping people.

- Esau wept when he realized he was tricked out of receiving his father's blessing. (Gen. 27:38)

- Joseph alternated between weeping and rejoicing as he saw how God was reuniting his family. (Gen. 45:1; 50:1)
- Hannah's prayers were so tear-filled and intense that the temple priest thought she was drunk. (1 Sam. 1:10–16)
- David wept with his men until he had no strength left to weep. (1 Sam. 30:4)
- Nehemiah, Job, Ezra, and Hezekiah wept as they prayed and interceded for others before the Lord. (Neh. 1:4; Job 30:25; Ezra 10:1; Isa. 38:3)
- Jesus grieved over Jerusalem because He knew how the people would reject His offer of salvation. (Matt. 23:37–39)
- Peter wept bitterly after he realized that he'd turned away from Jesus. (Matt. 26:75)
- The apostle Paul had a passionate desire to protect the church from false prophets, and this often left him in tears. (Acts 20:31)
- The apostle John wept when he saw a sealed scroll and noticed that no one on the earth was worthy to open it. (Rev. 5:3–4)

We don't have to clean ourselves up before we come to God with our feelings. David's psalms are filled with bold proclamations of sorrow, anger, and impatience before God. Both the book of Lamentations and the book of Job are filled with anguished, emotionally messy conversations with God. Jesus tells us to bring all our burdens to Him as a way to find rest from challenging emotions (Matt. 11:28–30).

Thankfully, God creates avenues for healing and repentance in the middle of our suffering and grief. Emotional turmoil can be an invitation to wrestle with God on the big questions, to feel His compassion, to grow in trust as release challenges, and depend on God for strength. For instance, sadness is an opportunity for God to restore us with His unmistakable comfort, and misunderstanding is an opportunity to dwell in the undeniable truth that we're fully known and accepted by Him.

Hard emotions may not be pleasant, but without opportunities to depend on Him in these times, how else could we access these deeper levels of intimacy with God? Like many of our Bible heroes, we can come to God tearstained and uncertain and know that He is eager to help us in our distress.

Truth #4: We Can Stand in Joy and Peace without Dismissing Uncomfortable Emotions

Christ has canceled our sin debt, blessed us with an irrevocable eternal inheritance, and promised to bring us eternal victory (Heb. 9:15). These truths can—and should—bring us God's strength in all circumstances, and they are definitely fodder for a grateful heart!

Yet our Savior has also warned us that we will experience trouble and pain in this world (John 16:33). If God expected us to live in the bliss of ongoing joy and peace, why would the Bible regularly emphasize our need for God's comfort? While God does allow us to live above our circumstances in joy and peace, He also gives us a living relationship with Him to help us uncover these gifts in a broken world full of understandably unpleasant emotions.

I recently heard a popular women's speaker say that complaining keeps us focused on a "poor me" attitude, when what we really need to do is stop whining and refocus our heart on godly joy. Yes, we must have hearts focused on God. The Bible also shares about how unbridled emotions can keep us stuck in a pity party, which makes our feelings our guide instead of God, but what if God wants to help us process what we're feeling *so that we can* fully rest in His joy?[4] Sometimes the road to the mountain of joy requires a willingness to sit with God in the valley of pain. God loves us too much to gloss over things that need to be dealt with, and sometimes our path to joy and peace requires that we courageously confront difficult emotional issues.

I experienced this when a male friend of mine made some comments that left me feeling uncomfortable. As a recovering people pleaser who avoids confrontation, my first response was to tell myself to stop feeling that way, dismiss it as my fault, and move on. It was the Holy Spirit, however, who would not let it go. He advocated for the little girl inside of me who had been wounded by men's comments in the past. I wasn't going to find solace until I spoke up on behalf of *her* feelings. It was an awkward conversation to have, but if I didn't address the comments then, the enemy would keep me locked in emotional turmoil and limit my ability to do ministry with this brother in Christ.

We can release any shame we have about not feeling joy in every season. Joy and peace are always ours in Christ, even when painful emotions cloud the happy feeling of these foundational truths. We can hold both joy and pain simultaneously as we authentically process complex experiences.

Truth #5: Emotions Are Real, but They Are Not God's Complete Truth

Emotions are a divine gift to help us understand ourselves and how we relate to the world, but they are greatly influenced by our internal biases and cognitive distortions. Yes, our feelings have merit, but we can't let our past shame tell a distorted story about our identity; we can't let our daily frustrations keep us from living in ongoing peace; and we can't let our future fears lie to us about God's ability to work all things together for our good and His glory (Rom. 8:28). When it comes to decision-making, our human emotions must always answer to God's unchanging truth as found in the Bible.

When my friend author Lisa Appelo unexpectedly became a widow and single mom to seven children, her emotional agony nearly derailed her spirit. Lisa spent the first few months after her husband's death in utter turmoil, spending hours each day crying and writing "God, I can't do this!" in her journal in large, capital letters. "Painful emotions will try to convince us that we will never smile again and that life will never be what we want it to be," she explained. "They will attempt to point out what God has withheld from us and can greatly skew our perspective of who God really is."[5]

We must continually be aware of how our emotions may tempt us to sin and to doubt God, especially His goodness, His plan, and His promises (Jer. 17:9). The enemy would love to use our emotions to create false perceptions about our relationships and distort our view of our worth as Christ's children. The enemy wants to turn our minds and emotions toward death and away from hope. We must stay alert to his schemes since our sinful nature is prone to listen to the voice of death and hopelessness. We can acknowledge our emotions, yet we must pay attention to how our individual emotional weaknesses can drive us away from God, even if that's one tiny millimeter at a time.

Truth #6: We Don't Have to Believe Everything We Think or Act on Everything We Feel

We are blessed with a thinking mind and a plethora of emotional responses. But we must remember that we get to choose what we will think about and decide whether or not we will act on those thoughts. There's a famous quote in psychology circles often attributed to Holocaust survivor Viktor Frankl: "Between stimulus and response there is a space. In that space is our power to choose our response. In our response lies our growth and our freedom."[6] By determining which thoughts we focus on, we get to decide which thought patterns we allow to be strengthened.

For example, we have permission to stop a thought pattern that opposes God's truth about our identity or His good plans for our future. Therefore, we can give ourselves permission not to act upon any emotion that leads us down a path of self-loathing, condemnation, or hopelessness since these don't align with God's perception of us.

Cognitive neuroscientist Dr. Caroline Leaf describes it this way: We have both a mind and a brain, which means we are given the ability to feel but also to analyze *what* we feel. We have the ability to stand outside our thoughts and decide what we will think about.[7] Talk about a superpower! It's true that pain makes it harder to discern truth and to decide what our best in-the-moment response should be, but even then, we still have the Holy Spirit's power to pause and decide how to respond.[8]

I often think of the mind as an air traffic controller who is in charge of our thoughts and emotions. Their job is to dictate if or when a plane can land on a given airfield. They have the authority to say, "You cannot land here," and the pilot must obey.

It's the same for our emotions and thoughts. We have the God-given authority to decide what our minds will allow to "land" in our sacred mental airfields. Because we have the mind of Christ, we have the authority to ask these "airplanes" to leave our proverbial airspaces if they don't belong there.

Have you ever heard the saying "No one else can make you feel inferior without your consent"?[9] The concept is 100 percent true. The enemy can't separate us from God's love, but he will do his darnedest to convince us that God's love is not real. We must be aware of what's happening in our minds and address any thought or feeling that opposes God's truth.

What does this look like in real life? As I worked on this chapter, my sixteen-year-old daughter texted me from class: "Mom, I feel so ugly right now. No one will ever like me." I first assured her that it's normal to feel this way sometimes, then I encouraged her to embrace her God-given responsibility to take charge of her thoughts and not let any lies form into false beliefs about herself. I reminded her that she's beautiful and that God has good plans for her life, but it's her choice to believe this truth or the enemy's lies. I also encouraged her to decide which thought pattern she was going to embrace.

Yes, we really *can* stop a thought pattern in its tracks and refuse to slide down an emotional spiral! It takes practice, and ADD—the emotional management tool we'll cover in part 2—is an excellent tool to help us navigate this process. Taking charge of our emotions starts, however, by first understanding that we have the responsibility and the authority to decide what we will focus on.

What are your biggest barriers to managing emotions well? You can download a printable list of these six truths from the link at the end of the chapter.

CHAPTER QUESTIONS

1. Which of these truths about emotions was most illuminating for you?
2. How have you seen God uniquely meet an emotional need in your life?
3. What insights did you learn from this chapter on why you struggle with processing emotions?

Testimonial

In the past I would express whatever emotion fit the situation without any self-control or boundaries. If I was upset, I would cry. If I felt angry, I would yell. If I was frustrated, I would sit in the pantry and eat.

Now I've learned to ask, Am I hearing this right? What's the truth here? I may have a good reason to feel angry, but that voice inside that's telling me to respond with anger or harshness is not from God, and so I'm learning not to lean on it.

Kimberly, coaching client

QUESTION

Are emotions sinful?

ANSWER

Our emotions can certainly affect our willingness to obey God. We are told to guard our heart, to not let our hearts be deceived, and to take every thought captive so as to better manage temptation and not step into sin (Ps. 139:23; 2 Cor. 10:5; Eph. 4:23). The Bible also advises us not to let the sun go down on our anger or to nurse hatred toward others in order to avoid sinful actions (Eph. 4:26; Lev. 19:17).

Further, Romans 8:6 encourages us to allow the Spirit to control our minds so that we can cultivate "life and peace."

God can use emotion to stir the hearts of His people *toward* obedience, further demonstrating that emotions themselves aren't sinful. Moses encouraged the Israelites to stay obedient to God by reminding them to view their emotionally challenging circumstances not with despair but with courage and bravery (Deut. 31:4–6).

Sometimes we can make an internal decision, such as to judge someone else or to look at them lustfully, and God considers those actions sin even if the outward manifestation of that decision never occurs. Jesus speaks of this concept in Matthew 5:28 when He says, "But I say, anyone who even looks at a woman with lust has already committed adultery with her in his heart" (NLT). In this situation it's important to note that previous thoughts, like "that person is really attractive," led to this sinful decision to lust. Since we are responsible for all our decisions, internal or external, it makes sense that Jesus would call it a sin.

Last, earlier in the chapter I shared how God the Father, Jesus, and the Holy Spirit demonstrate emotion. If emotions are inherently sinful, then it would be impossible for the members of the Trinity to exhibit unpleasant emotions like anger and sadness and still remain holy.

So, to answer the question, it's true that emotions and thoughts can lead us to make sinful decisions, but, no, emotions and thoughts are not sinful by themselves.

Don't forget to check out the free downloads for *Emotional Confidence*! There's a quiz, helpful exercises, and even audio and video tools to help you continue your journey in managing your emotions.

Go to AliciaMichelle.com/Emotional-Downloads to access these free resources.

4

Emotional Prep: 18 Ways to Calm the Body and Quiet the Mind

It was 3:00 a.m. My heart was racing, my hands were shaking, and I couldn't catch my breath. I was in a tiny New York City hotel room trapped in full-fledged panic mode.

The trip's activities and the hustle and bustle of everything around me converged to make me want to jump out of my skin. I was both nervous and ecstatic about my meetings with top producers and editors later that morning. I was also eager to make this a fun time of connection with my fifteen-year-old who'd traveled with me to New York for the first time, but I was exhausted from a full day of long car rides and even longer flights. To top it off, the crowded buildings and people everywhere were a stark contrast to my rural hometown life, which triggered an intense claustrophobia.

As I tossed and turned in bed early that morning, my soul circled for a place to find shelter yet turned up empty. I repeatedly told myself to relax, seeking logic as an avenue to peace.

Then I heard His loving whisper. *Jesus*, I thought. *Yes, Jesus! He is right here and hasn't left me.* My soul recounted God's assurances of His presence in times of trouble. I meditated on truths found in Psalm 139:7. *Where can I flee from Your presence? Where can I go where You are not, my awesome Savior?*

Despite my attempts to reflect on God's promises and convince myself that I was safe, calm wouldn't come. The intangible hysteria kept rising, which led to even more fear and overwhelm. I logically knew God was with me, but I was so locked in panic that His truths felt shallow and ineffective.

If you've ever experienced this kind of heart-wrenching distress, then you understand how agonizing it is to be so engulfed in anxiety that when truth is right in front of you, you still can't let it in!

Managing our emotions requires carefully listening to both our spirit and the Holy Spirit to help us move through heightened emotion. *What am I feeling? What do I need? How might He want to help me? What is He trying to draw my attention toward?* This is the heart of the ADD model, which we'll talk about in part 2.

When we're stuck in emotional overwhelm, however, strong feelings like anger and worry can cloud our vision and keep us emotionally frozen. We can know what to do logically and yet feel as powerless as a flailing branch being swept down a raging river.

This is when we need calming strategies to switch our mental and physical state from reactivity into receptivity. I call these essential calming tools and mindsets *emotional prep*, and in this chapter we'll talk about how to calm surface-level emotions so that we can effectively use the ADD method to process the root emotion.

The Emotional Iceberg and Amygdala Hijack

Have you ever been so mad that you can't think straight? Or felt so mentally or physically overwhelmed by a situation that it's not clear where to start? Psychologist John Gottman first coined the term *anger iceberg* as a way to describe how, like a physical iceberg, a person's anger is often only the "tip" of their emotions, with everything from sadness to loneliness to shame hiding below the surface.[1] This analogy is also called the *emotional iceberg* since feelings like overwhelm and anxiety can appear "above the surface."

Mental health professionals often use the emotional iceberg metaphor to help clients define what other emotions may be underneath their initial feelings and to create a helpful order for emotional processing. It can be extremely difficult to name and work through these tender "below the surface" emotions—commonly termed *secondary emotions*—when our minds are resounding with potent feelings like bitterness or fury. It's like our minds are crying out for relief in these areas so they can clearly process the deeper emotions and minister to the pain.

So why do our brains get stuck in these places where it feels like logical truth can't penetrate?

Let's look again to the amygdala, those two almond-shaped inner brain structures that are responsible for the fight-flight-freeze-please responses. Sudden emotional triggers, especially those rooted in fear and pain, can cause the amygdala to overreact so intensely that it literally shuts down the logical brain centers. The amygdala has "hijacked" the brain's responses, and only survival-based responses and emotions reign.[2]

Obviously, this amygdala hijacking dramatically affects how we respond to intense emotions in the moment. While there are universal responses during an amygdala hijacking, such as a quickening heartbeat, each individual experiences a unique reaction based on their triggers and past trauma.[3] Even the presence of certain mental health conditions, such as post-traumatic stress disorder or bipolar disorder, can affect the sensitivity and reactivity of a person's amygdala.[4]

I recently saw this varied amygdala hijack response on full display. Several friends and I had just pulled into a parking spot at a restaurant. As we exited the vehicle, a man in a pickup truck next to us suddenly leaped out of his vehicle. Our lively conversation instantly silenced when the man began hurling insults at us, insisting that we'd hit his truck with our vehicle door. He was extremely agitated and confrontational, especially toward my friend Tom who he believed hit his truck.

Interestingly, each of us had a different reaction to this man's aggressive behavior. I suddenly shut down, could not speak, and was near tears. In an instant I was a four-year-old girl, frozen in fear because she was caught off guard by a loved one's unexpected outburst. Tom had a similar response, as he could barely look the man in the eye and kept repeating "we didn't hit your car." My friend Julie's reaction was the most surprising. This gracious, always-smiling woman of God suddenly morphed into a frothing pit bull ready to take down an intruder. She marched her petite frame up to the enraged man, pointed her finger in his face, and shouted like a seasoned New York cabbie, "HEY! No one talks to my friends like that! Back OFF!"

Can you see the different manifestations of the fight-flight-freeze-please responses? Tom described that, due to past trauma, he couldn't even logically process what the man was saying, and his mind, body, and physical reactions were frozen (freeze response). Julie described that she'd always stepped in to confront anyone who was being unfairly treated without a speck of fear for the other person's reaction, so she faced off with this man without hesitation (fight response). As for me in that moment, I'd just wanted to find a hole to hide in since I was terrified of escalating the situation (flight response). I was also flooded with shame and guilt because I was horrified that I'd done something wrong to upset someone else (please response).[5]

Looking back, I can see that the barrier blocking me from experiencing truth that night I lay awake in my New York hotel room was the same factor at play that day in the parking lot with my friends and the agitated man. I was not able to process truth in either moment because my logical brain was offline, and my amygdala was calling the shots.

As we've established, when emotions feel especially heady, we need to first find calm so that we can find clarity. Fortunately, God designed our physical bodies to help us find relief from tumultuous emotions.

Amygdala Response

Response	Possible Thoughts	Potential Actions
Fight (explosion)	"I need to express these emotions right now and defend myself."	Yelling; screaming; attacking

Response	Possible Thoughts	Potential Actions
Flight (distraction)	"I need to numb myself, avoid, or run from these feelings."	Emotionally hiding or shutting down; leaving the situation; seeking pleasure/ distraction through TV, phone, food, etc.
Freeze (overthinking)	"I have no idea what to do. I'm emotionally stuck and spinning in overwhelm."	Indecision; racing thoughts; anxious what-if questions
Please (judgment)	"I need to silence these emotions because they will make me look bad or make me stick out."	Overediting or overanalyz- ing a response; pushing feelings down; condemn- ing/judging oneself for feeling a certain way; people-pleasing

Soothing the Chaos with the Parasympathetic Nervous System

Because lasting peace is a fruit of the Spirit that can only come from God, we cannot create it on our own. What we can do, however, is tap into God's peace by practicing specific actions that, biologically speaking, turn up the serenity and turn down the stress. How? Let's take a quick tour of how our nervous system affects our physical and emotional state.

The *autonomic nervous system* is an interconnected system of neurons that automatically receives information about the body and regulates the functioning of the various organs, including blood pressure, digestion, body temperature, heart rate, and breathing rate. This system functions as two parts: the *sympathetic nervous system* and the *parasympathetic nervous system*. Based on the data it receives, the autonomic nervous system determines whether to stimulate certain body processes (sympathetic) or to inhibit certain body processes (parasympathetic). For example, the amygdala's fight-flight-freeze-please reaction is a sympathetic nervous system response that prepares our body to physically defend itself.[6]

If our brain determines that our safety is at risk, our sympa- thetic nervous system prepares us for battle by increasing our heart rate, dilating our eyes, and increasing blood to the extremities. If our brain notices that danger is not present, however, the parasympathetic system keeps the body at homeostasis by conserving energy, restoring tissues, and eliminating waste.[7]

When the parasympathetic nervous system is activated, there's a sense of stillness, balance, and stability in the body and mind.[8] This is why the parasympathetic system is sometimes called the "rest and digest" state. Our breath pattern and quality are strong indicators of whether we're operating in the sympathetic state (shallow, quickened breaths) or parasympathetic state (deeper inhalations and exhalations).

Thankfully, we can learn to manually trigger our parasympathetic nervous system when experiencing high levels of stress. This relaxation response is another fantastic God-given power for managing our emotions. It's a much-needed bridge that allows us to honor the reality of an intense emotion while helping our body transition to a calmer mental state where we can better assess our internal discomfort.

To switch from the parasympathetic to the sympathetic system we must first notice *what* is going on in our bodies. When I was looking for relief during that middle-of-the-night panic attack in New York, I observed my body's shallow breathing, panicky thoughts, and restless energy as evidence of a sympathetic nervous state. While my emotions were too volatile to address at first, I started practicing a few of my tried-and-true parasympathetic coping strategies—visualization, lightly brushing my skin with my fingers, and box breathing—in order to eventually better examine what was happening mentally.

Once I felt relaxation settling in and my breathing returning to normal, I could hear God's voice more clearly. He encouraged me to seek wisdom and comfort in His Word so that I could further calm myself down. I grabbed my phone, walked into the bathroom, turned on the light, typed *calm* into an online Bible concordance, and began soaking in the verses. Then I was able to use ADD to process what was really going on and determine why I'd been so triggered. It took almost an hour to get back to sleep that night, but by God's grace, I woke up the next morning free from the inner chaos and ready to step into the day's excitement.

God has designed the calming parasympathetic state to be our body's default biological state,[9] and when we're suffering, He wants to help us get back into balance. What a blessing that we can invite God into each of these parasympathetic-stimulating processes, even when our warring emotions make His presence feel far away.

16 Ways to Switch Our Body to a Parasympathetic State

The purpose of emotional prep is to shift the nervous system from a reactive to a responsive state in order to best navigate "below the surface" emotions with a tool like ADD. There are an unlimited number of ways we can turn on the relaxation response through the parasympathetic nervous system. As you will see below, many involve our physical body, but some incorporate the spiritual and mental aspects of self as well.

Not only can we use these calming tools to welcome tranquility on the fly but we can also create a regular rhythm of practices that trigger the parasympathetic nervous system. These tools can be used individually or in combination to layer different calming remedies. Some of these may be a more natural fit than others, so experiment to see which are most effective for you.

1. Allow yourself to cry. Crying not only activates the parasympathetic nervous system, but emotional tears help detox the body of stress hormones.[10] It also releases pain-dulling endorphins like oxytocin into the bloodstream, which explains why the body may feel numb after crying. It may not feel like a calming activity while the tears are flowing, but there's no doubt that the body finds release through emotional tears.[11] Instead of bottling up your tears the next time you feel overwhelmed, lean into that emotional release and let them flow.

2. Pray. Perhaps it goes without saying but when overwhelming emotions build to a frenzy, take a moment to pray and ask God to intervene. Jesus sent us the Holy Spirit as a great comforter through all of life's ups and downs. And 1 John 3:20 reminds us that even if our emotions are intense, God's truth is greater than our feelings, and we can trust Him to guide us through what we're perceiving. Thankfully, prayer is available day or night!

3. Use a deep breathing method. Researchers at Northwestern University noted how neurons in the limbic system, including neurons in the amygdala and hippocampus, were stimulated during deep inhalation. They found that breathing, especially nasal breathing, not only increases oxygen in the body but also "creates electrical activity in the human brain that enhances emotional judgments and memory recall." Lead author and assistant professor of neurology Christina Zelano notes, "When you inhale, you are in a sense synchronizing brain oscillations across the limbic network."[12] Other research confirms the power of meditative breathing to invoke calm by lowering heart rate, decreasing blood pressure, and diffusing the fight-flight-freeze-please response.[13]

One of my favorite breathing techniques is *box breathing*, which involves breathing in for four counts, holding the breath for four counts, then breathing out for four counts and holding that breath for four counts. Two other powerful techniques shown to help reduce tension are *alternate nostril breathing* (alternately blocking one nostril and breathing through the other) and *lion's breath breathing* (inhaling through the nose and forcefully exhaling through an open mouth while making the "ha" sound and sticking the tongue out). No matter which breath pattern you choose, focus on deep inhalations through the nose that fill the belly and extended exhalations that empty the entire breath from the rib cage.

4. Meditate and visualize a soothing spiritual concept. Meditation and visualization turn on the "rest and digest" system by engaging the imagination to release tension and receive peace. Visualization comes in various forms, including reliving a happy memory, imagining problems floating by on a cloud, or envisioning oneself in an idealized setting, such as resting on a cliff overlooking the ocean.

While scientists have found meditation especially powerful when combined with deep breathing,[14] I've discovered that adding spiritual elements to a visualization—such as picturing Jesus's presence in the mental image—is extremely beneficial in high-stress situations. Consider bringing Scripture meditation to a visualization practice by imagining what a spiritual concept or Bible verse might actually look like. For example, I like to imagine Psalm 23 coming to life as Jesus leads me beside the peaceful stream of a waterfall and invites me to rest with Him in the nearby grass as we appreciate the natural beauty of the flowers and trees.

Download the meditation video and audio tool from Isaiah 26:3 found at the link at the end of this chapter if you'd like to try this combination of breathing, visualization, and Scripture meditation together. This meditation is only five to seven minutes long, making it an easy way to fit meditation into your busy lifestyle.

5. **Reduce any outside stimuli.** The greater the external stimuli, the more likely it will trigger the sympathetic nervous system. (You know, the chaotic overwhelm of a kids-screaming, food-burning, dog-barking, "Mommy's going to lose it" moment). In the heat of the heightened feeling, you can calm visual, auditory, or physical stimuli by closing your eyes and "going" somewhere to seek solace where there's little noise or stimulation. Regular rhythms of silence and solitude are especially great for kick-starting the parasympathetic response and are essential during high-stress life seasons, such as walking with a loved one through terminal illness. This is especially true for those *highly sensitive persons* who have an increased ability to process larger amounts of sensory information—a blessing for relationship connection but an added resistance when attempting to calm overwhelm or anger.[15] Whether He was highly sensitive or not, Jesus often found it restorative to retreat to a quiet place, so why not heed His example.

6. **Use a weighted blanket.** Speaking of sensory stimulation, *sensory integration theory* suggests deep pressure calms the nervous system.[16] This is why many find it helpful to use a weighted blanket when stress levels rise. Oncology nurses at a cancer institute noted how weighted blankets used during infusion treatments lowered patient anxiety levels.[17] Weighted blankets have also been known to encourage better sleep and to provide anxiety relief for those with sensory-processing disorders or autism.[18] Some suggest that

the heaviness of a weighted blanket feels similar to a hug, and this contributes to its therapeutic benefits. My family and I regularly sleep with weighted blankets, especially during anxious or stressful seasons. Whether at nighttime or throughout the day, experiment with using a weighted blanket to soothe your nervous system.

7. Try progressive muscle relaxation or deep muscle relaxation. *Progressive muscle relaxation* (PMR) is done by noticing different parts of the body and inviting each segment to first tense up and then to relax. PMR has long been proven to help reduce stress and anxiety,[19] so it's a powerful tool for turning on the parasympathetic nervous system and releasing psychological as well as physiological tension. *Deep muscle relaxation* (DMR) is a shortened version of PMR where the entire body is invited to relax all at once.

Here's a simple way to practice PMR or DMR: Find a quiet place, lie down, and get comfortable. Starting at the top of the head, imagine a warm ray of healing light slowly scanning down each segment of the body. Imagine that this light is bringing release and relaxation to every place it touches. As the light illuminates each section of the body, exhale and relax that area completely, allowing the tension to seep out of the muscles. While we may not be able to practice PMR or DMR at any given moment, they are excellent stress-management strategies that calm a panicky feeling and make the body less likely to jump into the sympathetic response when triggered.

8. Lightly touch your skin. When I was a little girl, I would beg my mom to let me lie across her lap while she ran her fingertips on my back, a practice we called *mousy-mousy*. As embarrassing as the name is, my kids are very familiar with mousy-mousy and asked for it all the time when they were younger. (Shh, don't tell—a few of my teens still request it.)

Why does light touch on the skin invite relaxation and switch on the parasympathetic response? Gentle touch stimulates nerve receptors in the skin called *c-tactile afferents* (CTs), which are known to spark pleasure centers in the brain, increase feelings of empathy, and start the flow of the relationship-bonding hormone oxytocin.[20] While this type of touch can be especially powerful when given by others with whom we have deep connection, the relaxation effect is still prevalent when practiced solo. Note: This technique is not recommended for those with sunburn, sensitive skin conditions, or inflammatory pain or other conditions where light touch brings irritation.

9. Use essential oils.[21] Whether inhaled or applied to the skin topically, several scientific studies demonstrate the effect that essential oils have on the nervous system. Lavender, chamomile, bergamot, sweet orange, anise, and geranium have been shown to reduce depression, and lavender, bergamot, and lemon balm have an analgesic effect.[22] One study demonstrated how lavender aromatherapy reduced preoperative anxiety in surgery patients.[23]

10. Check in on your physical well-being. When feeling extra emotionally triggered, it's wise to quickly check in on our body's basic needs. We often push ourselves too hard, eat poorly, and ignore our physical needs for rest, and this inflames how we emotionally respond to life's challenges. For instance, hunger, low blood sugar, dehydration, and lack of sleep can make us more emotionally reactive. I once saw a sign outside a coffee shop that read "I'm sorry for what I said when I was hungry and caffeine-deprived." Yep, the struggle is real.

When I notice myself more on edge and unable to handle life's everyday problems, I ask myself three questions: (1) Have I recently eaten something nutritious that will stabilize my blood sugar? (2) Have I had enough water today? and (3) How's my sleep been over the past week?

11. Move the stress out of your body with physical exercise. Physical exercise is one of the best tools when energy needs to be released. This could be strenuous exertion like running, swimming, or hiking—anything that causes the heart rate to elevate. Yoga and gentle stretching can be helpful options as well.

Whether done in the moment to release pent-up energy or done as part of a daily routine, the link between physical exercise and good mental health is undeniable and well proven. Aerobic exercise encourages *neurogenesis*—the creation of new brain cells—and exercise increases the level of mood-regulating neurotransmitters like serotonin, dopamine, and norepinephrine.[24] I see a night-and-day difference in my ability to navigate my emotions when I stay on my morning routine of walking, yoga, or Pilates. But when I skip exercise for several days, I feel more tense and emotionally charged up, almost like static electricity has built inside of me. Get moving when you need to release emotional energy.

12. Change position or location. Behavioral scientist Amy Hale noted that our body's physiology changes as we switch environments and that we can use this to our advantage to discover refreshment when stress looms.[25] When I felt emotionally overwhelmed and overstimulated as a stay-at-home mom of littles, one of my tried-and-true strategies was to pile the kids in the car and switch up our surroundings. A quick run to the store or even a walk through the neighborhood got me out of my head and emotionally reset my kids too as we typically were all much calmer (and nicer to each other) when we got home. Now I utilize this technique on the days when I'm feeling creatively stuck or overwhelmed by my to-do list.

13. Get out in nature or listen to nature sounds. Getting into nature can have an immediate calming effect on the body. Interestingly, researchers found that people who live in green spaces and who regularly spend time in nature use fewer prescription drugs for both their physical and mental health.[26]

Studies show that being near water—especially beach areas—helps switch on the parasympathetic system. Watching and hearing the ebb and flow of the surf encourages our brain to recalibrate from high-energy beta brain waves found in our normal waking state to alpha and theta brain waves found when we are deeply relaxed or sleeping. Combine this with the calming blue of the water, a higher level of oxygenated air at the shoreline, and the beautiful scenery, and it makes sense why we feel especially relaxed after a day near the water.[27] If we can't escape to the great outdoors, even listening to nature sounds is scientifically proven to bring calm to our minds.[28] Consider listening to a nature-themed playlist the next time your body needs tranquility.

14. Engage the brain differently. Although it seems counterintuitive, unpleasant physical stimuli can be a powerful way to recalibrate the brain. These types of exercises act as a mental grounding, switching the brain out of fight-flight-freeze-please mode. Some techniques include holding an ice cube in the hand or snapping a rubber band against the wrist. The discomfort of the cold or the snap of a rubber band triggers a pain response, which causes the neurotransmitters to refocus on the sensation. We can also engage a different part of the brain by doing a quick math problem, counting backward from one hundred by twos, or, if a person is bilingual, translating text from one language to another. These techniques are not for everyone, but for some they're a powerful way to switch the brain out of the sympathetic and into the parasympathetic state. Give them a try to see if they're a fit for you.

15. Practice a calming response to the trigger. If we find ourselves being triggered by the same stimuli, we can create a short, responsive statement or action that placates our anger, overwhelm, or worry and reminds us, first, that we're going to be all right, and, second, that we have tools to release the heightened feeling. For example, we can repeat a short phrase like "I'm safe," "God is with me," or "it's understandable but with God's help, I can stay calm" when emotions flare. You could write this down on a card and keep it in a handy spot, like a digital note on your phone or a Post-it on your mirror.

Another example of a practiced response is to picture a door slamming shut to block a rabbit trail of out-of-control thoughts from running amok in your mind or closing your eyes and opening your hands palms-up to signify the emotions leaving your body. Whether you recite a short phrase or replay a visual, see how these responses could bring peace around ongoing stressful stimuli.

16. Listen to music that brings calm or helps you release emotion. Research proves that music can enliven or calm our emotions. Music therapy has been effective for those struggling with depression, and it aids in reducing anxiety and stress in heart disease patients.[29]

Several studies also indicate that a person's positive connection with music is more important than the specific music type.[30] In other words, one person may find it calming to blast eighties metal rock while another plays Bach's *Concerto for Two Violins* to reset their soul. Praise and worship music can have an especially powerful benefit because it allows us to focus on God's presence and refocus our mind on spiritual truth. Create a calm-themed playlist for yourself and experiment with how different genres affect your mood.

Now That We've Found Calm . . .

Anger, overwhelm, and worry are feelings that deserve our attention, and in this chapter, we've established some practical ways to soothe these intense emotions. To find true emotional resolution, however, we must also ask what's going on underneath those surface-level feelings. That's where ADD comes in, and that's where we're headed in part 2!

CHAPTER QUESTIONS

1. Have you ever found yourself so emotionally upset that you weren't sure how to find calm? If so, what did you do, and was it helpful?
2. What are some of your body's signs that the sympathetic fight-or-flight response has taken over?
3. Which of the sixteen emotional prep tools will you try the next time you feel emotionally triggered and need to find calm before processing what's going on inside?

Testimonial

When I'm too fired up to even acknowledge what I'm feeling, I know I need to use an emotional prep tool: to step outside a second, do some box breathing, or check to see when I ate last. If I'm really stressed, I'll listen to loud music and even scream it out. If I sense that my anger is about to get the best of me and I am no longer able to use ADD rationally, then I give myself permission to step away and cool off, and it's made a big difference in my ability to manage my moods.

Micah, Christian Mindset Makeover course participant

QUESTION

What about emotional eating? Is it okay to use food to calm myself down?

ANSWER

There are many biological and cultural reasons why we're drawn to use food to comfort challenging emotions. Even as infants, God allows us to use food as a positive way to help regulate emotions. "A crying baby is designed to be comforted through the milk from a bottle or a mother's breast," Katrina Sequenzia, certified integrative nutrition health coach and registered nurse, told me in episode 207 of *The Christian Mindset Coach* podcast. "Emotional eating is simply a part of being human."[31]

Even if it's more fast food than a fantastic feast, God gives us the opportunity to enjoy the pleasurable aroma, texture, and taste of food at least three times a day. Food is at the center of many celebrations with friends and family, including birthdays, Thanksgiving, and Christmas. Jesus often gathered with His disciples over a meal, and the Bible even mentions that we'll be feasting in heaven (Luke 14:15).

However, food is meant to be enjoyed in a way that honors God. Emotional eating can become problematic when food becomes a coping mechanism or a way to escape pain. Just like the enemy wants to corrupt the gift of sex through pornography, he wants to twist God's good gift of food into an opportunity for idolatry. Do we find ourselves eating in isolation or hiding what we're eating from others? Do we turn to food when we're feeling down or troubled? Metaphorically speaking, are we eating in the dark or in the light?

Katrina notes that unhealthy emotional eating often starts in childhood or early adulthood as we often don't have the maturity to process big emotions in these life stages. Food can be a quick and instant tool to soften painful emotions in the moment.

We can begin a healthier relationship with food by mindfully discerning *why* we're reaching for that vanilla-ice-cream-covered brownie. Remember, the issue isn't the brownie itself—I'm thankful for this, because I'm quite a fan of brownies—but whether we're using the brownie to escape the bad or to savor the good.

Don't forget to check out the free downloads for *Emotional Confidence*! There's a quiz, helpful exercises, and even audio and video tools to help you continue your journey in managing your emotions.

Go to AliciaMichelle.com/Emotional-Downloads to access these free resources.

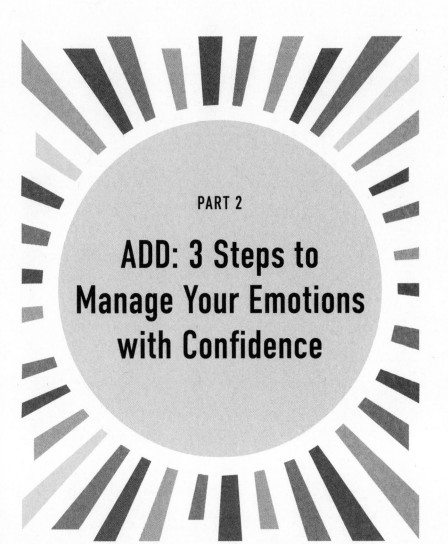

PART 2

ADD: 3 Steps to Manage Your Emotions with Confidence

5

What Is ADD?

I love gazing out the window of a plane to see the ground below, especially when the plane is about to land and the city landmarks are recognizable. I find this thirty-thousand-foot view extremely helpful for creating a mental map of where I'm about to disembark and what I'm about to encounter.

We're starting our discussion of ADD from this same bird's-eye view perspective. It's important that we have a clear understanding of the entire process so that we don't allow the craggy terrain of a specific emotion, the dense thicket of painful memories, or the vast prairies of immobilizing fears to detract us from reaching the overall destination.

ADD's goal is holy reconciliation between the realities of emotion and truth. We'll discover that this powerful emotional management tool helps us cultivate emotional confidence because it's a concrete, step-by-step process that invites us to partner with God as we navigate tricky feelings.

ADD: A Powerful Three-Step Emotional Management Tool

Let's start by breaking down each aspect of ADD step-by-step:

1. *Acknowledge*: We notice what we're feeling through God's loving filter of compassion.

2. *Discern*: We examine our emotions through God's clarifying lens of truth.

3. *Decide*: We courageously choose a God-honoring response to our feelings and determine where to emotionally dwell.

How can we respond to our feelings in a way that honors both their validity and the truths of God? We start with noticing (*acknowledge*), move to introspection (*discern*), and then to action (*decide*). This simple three-step flow is a foundational emotional management skill that brings calm, clarity, and control back to chaotic feelings.

I liken the ADD process to the steps of organizing a cluttered room. As we first pull everything out of the space, we acknowledge every part of the room's contents, asking ourselves, What's here? What are we dealing with? Next, we examine the contents themselves, categorizing trash from treasure and considering, Which items do we want to keep? What do we not need moving forward? Last, we choose what we will place back into the room and how we will arrange the contents as we determine, Which aspect of the room will serve as the focal point? How can we arrange the room's contents in a way that doesn't hide its limitations but directs our attention toward the brightest corners?

ADD is not a miracle cure that ties nice, neat bows on life's problems; instead, it's a flexible framework that offers a stable, proven structure for harmonizing feelings with facts. ADD is a tool for leaning into the tension between truth and emotion in order to discover previously unknown, hope-filled perspectives.

ADD allows us to hold space for the imperfect in order that the perfect healing of Christ may emerge.

Rooted in Science and Scripture

In previous chapters we shared a lot of scientific information behind how our mind works in relationship to our emotions, and we can remember these concepts as we look at the ADD model. For instance, both neuroscience and the Bible concur that if we want to change our behavioral response, we must first change the thoughts and emotions behind the behavior. Brain science demonstrates that we have the *power* to control our thoughts and emotions, while verses like Romans 12:1–2 indicate that we have a *responsibility* to manage our minds as part of our worshipful, sacrificial response to salvation.

How else does the Bible support the ADD model? To begin, verses like Psalm 139:23–24 model the ADD pattern: "Search me, God, and know my heart" (*acknowledge*); "test me and know my anxious thoughts. See if there is any offensive way in me" (*discern*); and "lead me in the way everlasting" (*decide*).

Psalm 12:1–8 is an example of how David's paradigm for processing emotions mirrors that of ADD. First, David *acknowledged* his feelings of frustration (vv. 1–4); second, he *discerned* what truths he knew about God in reference to the situation (vv. 5–6); and third, he *decided* on a new course of action by committing to a godly mindset of trust (vv. 7–8). David often repeats this sequence within a single psalm as he reconciles his emotions with the truths of God to determine his response to his troubles (Pss. 22; 56).

Job also followed a similar model of acknowledging his pain, discerning truth, and deciding how to manage his extremely difficult circumstances as he spoke freely with God (Job 24; 29; 30; 31). In 2 Kings 19, King Hezekiah worked with God to manage his anger and feelings of helplessness about the threat of invasion from the Assyrians by first bringing his pain to light (vv. 1–4); processing truth before God (vv. 14–18); and comforting himself and releasing his frustration by reflecting on God's authority (v. 19).

A Closer Look at Acknowledge, Discern, and Decide

Let's look closer to see the biblical and scientific evidence for each step of ADD.

1. Acknowledge

Since both the Bible and science show that we can't fully hide our feelings from ourselves or from God, honesty is a critical element for managing chaotic emotions. It requires vulnerable acknowledgment of what's true. I've witnessed firsthand in my coaching practice how the subconscious mind shuts down and goes into protection mode when we outright deny our emotions or try to logically convince ourselves of a truth while still holding unprocessed pain or doubt. As we learned, our amygdala can move into fight-or-flight mode anytime it senses a potential threat. This is why healthy emotional processing must begin with *acknowledging* the full reality of a situation. The Psalms give several examples of how David's honest acknowledgment of his thoughts and emotions were an important aspect of both his spiritual growth and his internal processing.

While we can see the scriptural importance of vulnerably acknowledging emotions, other Bible stories reveal another important element in the process: loving compassion. We are called to model Jesus's example of how to interact with others. As a loving God who cares for His children, Jesus acknowledged others with kindness and loving compassion (Mark 6:34). Even when He was issuing a painful correction, His "tough love" conviction was never condemning or offered without hope for change (John 8:11). God, who is described as "the Father of compassion," extends His loving compassion to His children in their time of need (2 Cor. 1:3). Instead of chastising or ignoring us, He is the perfect embodiment of love Paul describes in 1 Corinthians 13. Even though our emotions ultimately have to submit to God's authority, we can still adopt a caring, kind approach to acknowledging what we're feeling.

Acknowledgment is a recognition of how the prevailing feeling has manifested in all parts of the self, including our thoughts (intellectual self), body sensations (physical self), and relationship with God (spiritual self). As previously shared, science confirms that each part of our self is interconnected and thus affected by the others. The Bible also recognizes this connection, encouraging us to love God with every part of ourselves, which signifies that each part plays a role in our emotional response not only to God but to all parts of life (Mark 12:30).

Once we take this first step toward vulnerably acknowledging our feelings, we can move on to discerning what we're feeling in light of truth.

2. Discern

Next, we must separate truth from lies so we can *discern* where to place our mental focus. Christ often helped others notice something they could not see for themselves or had been refusing to acknowledge, which is why discernment utilizes biblical truth and Holy Spirit listening as the "plumb line" for gaining self-awareness to manage emotions.

How does *discernment* work? First and foremost, we should be discerning Scripture's perspective on our emotional response to a situation. However, we should also be asking for God's wisdom on how an emotion may be related to deeper core needs (like the ones mentioned in chap. 2), to past experiences, or to future fears. While we as Christ followers are tasked with the often-daunting responsibility of transparent emotional processing, God has equipped us with the mind of Christ to know what truth is and the gift of the Holy Spirit as our comforter (John 14:16–17).

Discernment is an active process, not a passive one. As we dig deeper into ADD and the *discern* step, we'll discover how to not only identify truth but how to actively choose to *stop* focusing on lies. Scripture encourages Christians to "destroy every proud obstacle that keeps people from knowing God" and to "capture their rebellious thoughts and teach them to obey Christ" in order to purify themselves and cultivate a Christ-honoring life (2 Cor. 10:5 NLT). Christians are also called to "love the Lord your God with all your heart and with all your mind and with all your soul" and to think about things that please the Spirit by letting the Spirit control our minds (Matt. 22:37; Rom. 8:5–6). Along with helping us understand and process emotions, discerning truth from lies is an important part of our ongoing sanctification and ability to cultivate a thriving relationship with Christ.

In order to discern truth from lies, we must continually fill our hearts with wisdom by practicing daily spiritual disciplines, such as Bible reading and prayer, that allow us to remain plugged into the vine and planted by His nourishing "stream" of living truth (Ps. 1:3). In later chapters we'll talk more about how to cultivate this type of dynamic spiritual growth through an authentic daily encounter with Christ.

3. Decide

The Bible states that we are to let God's truth—not the up-and-down nature of our emotions—be our solid anchor for decision-making (James 1:5–6). However, there's a difference between noticing truth and acting in truth. *Decide* provides the opportunity to move forward by actively choosing a new mindset that has been reconciled with the honesty of our emotions and our need to obey God's direction.

God allows space for emotional wrestling as we walk through decision-making, and this is emphasized in the *decide* step. Jesus experienced this internal conflict Himself the night before the crucifixion. He was so emotionally distraught about His call to the cross that He sweat drops of blood—a physical manifestation of His intense emotions. Jesus utilized prayer as a tool for both authentic reflection and spiritual discernment for His decision, specifically stating that His desire was not His own will, but that God's will be done (Matt. 26:39). From this incredible scene it's clear that God gives us permission to openly wrestle with truth and emotions as long as our ultimate desire is to do His will.

Inner confidence and lasting peace are hallmark signs of a heart that's taken the time to process emotions in light of biblical wisdom. Like Jesus in the garden, *decide* is our opportunity to reflect on the reality of a situation in light of God's will and to choose obedience as our ultimate act of love and submission to our Creator. We can submit to God's truth and yet know that God still sees and holds our emotional anguish. *Decide* gives us the chance to rise above our pain without negating it.

How to Use ADD

Since each step in ADD plays a unique role in emotional processing, it's important we move carefully and conscientiously through them all, always starting with the *acknowledge* step. It can take under a minute to move through the stages, or it can take months depending on the depth of the emotion or the longevity of the situation. Much like the nonlinear five stages of grief, we can jump back and forth between *acknowledge* and *discern* before we get to *decide*, and that's okay.

I've found it helpful to picture the ADD process like a spinning wheel (see the figure above). *Acknowledge*, *discern*, and *decide* are key points on the wheel, and we utilize specific tools, such as introspective questions and statement prompts (which we'll detail in future chapters), to keep the flow going and the wheel turning. Regular use fuels the momentum and makes it easier for ADD to become a mental habit that lowers stress and invites calm when emotions flare. In future chapters we'll share how to dig deeper into ADD, including how to apply the process to specific emotions and cultivate habits that make it easier to practice.

ADD can be used to manage emotions in the moment, to process several ongoing emotions related to a single issue, or to check in with our emotional self as part of a regular self-care routine. No matter how you utilize this tool, you'll notice how it becomes second nature the more it's practiced. And take heart: whether working through your feelings feels foreign or familiar, ADD is a learned life skill that anyone can utilize for more mental clarity.

The ADD Flow

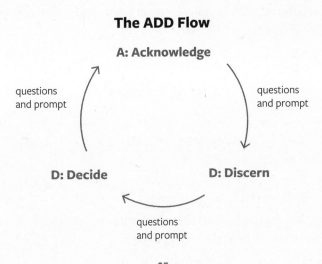

A: Acknowledge

questions
and prompt

questions
and prompt

D: Decide

D: Discern

questions
and prompt

It's important to keep in mind that not every emotional quandary will have an immediate resolution. I understand—waiting for emotional resolution is never easy. When we've worked through the steps and still feel uncertain or lack peace, we can relax knowing that we're held in this moment and that further revelation is coming. Sometimes we need to step away from an especially intense emotion and ground ourselves in God's comforting love as we sort through what we're feeling and what to do next. We can also use the calming techniques from chapter 4 as we release the outcome and wait for God to speak. Should the emotional tension arise again, which is highly likely since the feelings are rattling around in our subconscious, we can check in with God and begin to walk through the ADD steps again, pausing in those areas that feel most therapeutic.

ADD's goal is to provide clarity and connection with Christ as we navigate challenging emotions in light of Scripture. Each step is a chance to partner with God to lovingly care for ourselves while shining His light with wise, kind, courageous responses to difficult situations. The true gold of ADD is not just insight and wisdom for managing hard situations but the blessings of priceless connection with God and the gift of self-awareness.

All right, enough chatting *about* ADD. It's time to move into experimentation and application! Let's dive deeper into *acknowledge*, the first step of the ADD flow.

CHAPTER QUESTIONS

1. Does processing emotions feel familiar or foreign to you? What have you experienced in the past when working through your feelings?
2. What fears or concerns come up when you think about working through emotions?
3. Which aspects of ADD are you most excited to try? Which are you most apprehensive to try?

Testimonial

ADD is so much more helpful than just telling ourselves to "stop thinking" something. Before I had ADD, I would wonder, How do I make myself "just believe" God's truth in an emotional moment like so many people advise when my feelings are also so real? *I understand that we're supposed to take any thoughts captive that don't align with God's thoughts, but if we don't deal with the feelings directly, then we're just stuffing them. I've used other tools to try to calm my feelings, but ADD gives me a proactive response to an emotion. It's so helpful for me to know what to do with the thought. I'm someone who needs structure, and ADD gives me a specific way to manage my emotions that really works!*

Nicki, coaching client

Don't forget to check out the free downloads for *Emotional Confidence*! There's a quiz, helpful exercises, and even audio and video tools to help you continue your journey in managing your emotions.

Go to AliciaMichelle.com/Emotional-Downloads to access these free resources.

6

A Is for Acknowledge

Have you ever watched the movie *Titanic*, the epic retelling of the "unsinkable" ocean liner's tragic fate? As the frigid water quietly and callously engulfs the luxury cruise ship, passengers display the full gamut of human emotion—everything from the sheer terror of those who rushed the lifeboats to the eerily calm acceptance of those like millionaire Benjamin Guggenheim who famously quipped, "We've dressed up in our best and are prepared to go down like gentlemen."[1]

Even though our emotional responses are typically not linked to life-or-death situations like those of the *Titanic* passengers, we are regularly given the opportunity to decide how we will manage the rising tide of our reasonable yet difficult-to-process responses to a broken world.

Recognizing the difficulty—in all its entirety—is the first step to managing heart-wrenching feelings well.

What Is Acknowledge and Why Is It Important?

Ignorance may be bliss, as the saying goes, but emotional restoration begins with a straightforward assessment of what is. That's why *acknowledge* is the first step in the ADD method.

When we *acknowledge*, we admit that the emotion we are feeling is real, explore what the emotion is about, and recognize why it's reasonable to feel the way we do. We give ourselves space to process, to feel, and to grieve what is broken or not right. *Acknowledge* invites detached curiosity—meaning we can explore the emotions without judgment—to help us rest in God's gift of compassion and plausibility.

Acknowledge does not remedy the frustrating emotion. It's a stage of recognition and empathy. *Acknowledge* is a place to be held and loved by God as He helps us honestly ascertain what's happening.

In her study on the book of Genesis, author Jen Wilkin notes that the first thing God does to bring order out of chaos in the creation account is create light.[2] That's what we're doing in the *acknowledge* stage—turning on the proverbial light inside our emotional turmoil and respectfully surveying the scene.

Acknowledge's main goal is to answer these two questions:

What thoughts and emotions am I experiencing?
Why does it make sense that I'm experiencing them?

Using the emotional iceberg analogy from chapter 4, we can notice both the surface-level emotions, like anger, and the secondary emotions that may be more hidden, like loneliness or disappointment. By the way, it's all right if those surface-level emotions make it feel impossible to see any other emotions at this step. Sometimes these secondary feelings become more apparent as we further analyze our feelings in the *discern* step.

It's okay to be honest with ourselves about what we discover, even though it's natural to want to hide our not-so-pretty parts as a form of self-protection. Even if we push certain feelings down, the emotion is real, whether or not we acknowledge it. Like an aching, infected tooth, if we want the discomfort to stop, we first have to recognize that the pain exists before we can do something about it.

The ADD Flow

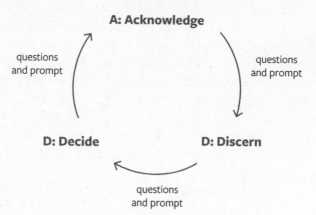

A: Acknowledge

questions
and prompt

questions
and prompt

D: Decide

D: Discern

questions
and prompt

Acknowledge
Questions:
• What thoughts and emotions am I experiencing?
• Why does it make sense that I'm experiencing them?
Prompt: "It makes sense that I'm feeling [X emotion] because of [Y situation]."
Caution: Watch out for the inner critic.

When we shame ourselves for our feelings, it's extremely difficult to move forward in vulnerability and bravery. That's why it's critical that we observe our emotions from a neutral, nonjudgmental stance. It may be tempting to become annoyed with ourselves for feeling a certain way, but neuroscience shows that self-judgment can create toxic patterns of emotional dysfunction, which eventually immobilize us from making courageous choices that bring wholeness.[3]

It's also extremely hard to process truth when we haven't adequately acknowledged the pain of our feelings. In the book of Job, Job loses his property, his livestock, and his children in one day, so naturally he is overcome with misery and grief. Job's friends immediately try to cheer Job up by reminding him that God will help him and that perhaps he needs to "consider the joy of those corrected by God" (5:17 NLT). Job first needed his pain and misery to be heard and acknowledged before he could begin to process God's truth, and I believe this is one reason why Job received his friends' words as harmful instead of helpful (6:25–30; 7:11–16).

We may be tempted to push painful emotions away without giving space for the feelings to be recognized, but stroke victim Katherine Wolf echoes the importance of first acknowledging pain when we're suffering. "When someone is not sure how they're going to get out of bed tomorrow, they don't need to hear 'You got this!' They need to hear, 'I can't believe this has happened to your life. I am so sorry.' The ministry of truth comes later. Give the ministry of tears and let people cry. . . . That is what they really need."[4]

Listen, I'm not advocating that our emotions should run wild and unchecked against truth. Nor am I saying that every emotion is in line with the Holy Spirit and should be acted upon. In *acknowledge* we're simply allowing our mind to see that the emotion is a reasonable response to the situation so that the mind can eventually absorb truth in the next step, *discern*. We can't seek godly wisdom and discern truth from lies until we've allowed ourselves to first honor the frustration through sincere acknowledgment.

The *acknowledge* step also allows us to recognize ongoing emotional patterns such as perfectionism or people-pleasing. We can notice how current emotions might be the result of past trauma or ongoing fears and draw helpful parallels for the *discern* and *decide* steps.

What Is God's Role in Acknowledge?

God is our supportive, caring ally through every stage of ADD, and in the *acknowledge* step, He offers His loving compassion so we can examine our feelings through the lens of His mercy. He gives us sympathy and space to process. With Him we have a partner who grasps our pain, and in the heat of the moment, this can make all the difference.

As one who experienced this world through a frail human frame, Jesus knows the heaviness of emotions and doesn't dismiss our pain as trivial. In the story of sisters Mary and Martha, Jesus lovingly convicts Martha about how she allowed the stress of taking care of everyone's needs to hinder her ability to focus on what's important in life (Luke 10:38–42 NLT). Interestingly, however, Jesus doesn't chastise Martha for wanting to be hospitable or for wanting to work hard to serve others. He compassionately lets her know that He notices her frustration and even uses "dear Martha" as a term of endearment. He acknowledges her stress and worry before He advises her on a solution.

God not only helps us identify our challenging feelings, but He also calms the emotions with His presence and brings solace by standing with us in the difficulty. In another story involving Mary and Martha, Jesus acknowledges and immerses Himself in these sisters' grief when their brother Lazarus dies (John 11:33–36).

And we can't forget the story of the pregnant Hagar crying in the desert after being kicked out of Abram and Sarai's home. The angel of the Lord, which some scholars believe to be the preincarnate Christ,[5] comforts her in her sorrow, and she responds by saying "you are the God who sees me" (Gen. 16:13).

Why is it critical that we know God as the great Comforter who walks with us through every emotional depth? Because, as we discussed previously, we are a people wired to be seen, known, and heard, especially in this era of cancel culture and gaslighting. When we understand that God recognizes our pain and see that we're not alone in the struggle, our defenses come down, our heightened feelings are calmed, and we can more readily accept our emotions.

Why Acknowledge Is Critical for Emotional Confidence

If you feel apprehensive about acknowledging emotions, I get it! Doing so hasn't come naturally for this logic-driven, type A woman either. I am that person who just wants things fixed and doesn't want to have to sit in a meadow holding hands with my inner child in order to get there.

But I've grown to love *acknowledge* because, surprisingly, I see the radical difference it's made in my ability to build authentic joy and genuine emotional confidence in my everyday life. It may feel counterintuitive that looking difficult emotions squarely in the eye can lead to a much-desired and highly elusive state of peace, but over and over I've found it to be true.

With God at our side, genuine acknowledgment also becomes an important tool in spiritual formation, godly confidence, and even sharing the gospel. When we recognize that God accepts us despite our messiest moods, we are free to grow into our best selves.

When difficult emotions cause us to doubt our sanity, we can think, *Hey, maybe I can learn to be patient with and love myself because that's how God relates to me.* Instead of masking our feelings, we can vulnerably say, *I'm really upset by this, and that's okay,* and gain courage to face even the most overwhelming emotions.

Vulnerable acknowledgment is frightening when viewed through a harsh, judgmental lens. But hallelujah that, in the *acknowledge* step, God gives us space to curiously explore our feelings within the context of His unstoppable love and acceptance! We can boldly emerge from the darkness and stand confidently in His healing light with all our scars on full display. What a difference that makes in every aspect of life!

2 Common Fears about Acknowledging Emotions

Does acknowledging emotions still feel a bit scary? Maybe you're thinking, *That all sounds great, but can't I skip this part and just make myself believe God's truth?* Let's talk about why that sentiment is understandable and what may be hiding behind a desire to skip over this important yet potentially awkward step.

Uncomfortable emotions are not the enemy. It can be tempting to respond to triggering situations from a one-dimensional, robotic perspective that avoids emotion, but our feelings give us variety and depth as we move through life.

We can't forget that emotions like fear or anxiety are normal responses to any new situation, especially one that feels risky—there's that amygdala again. In the same way that God's grace allows us to transparently acknowledge our feelings, we can freely name our concerns about processing emotions without shame.

Let's discuss two common fears that distort our perspective of the *acknowledge* step and make us apprehensive about jumping in with both feet.

Fear #1: "My feelings already seem out of control, so why would I focus on them more?"

I don't want to admit that I'm broken. None of us do! I am constantly seeking to better myself and it can seem like fixating on my weaknesses will somehow sabotage my growth. In other words, I fear that if I acknowledge my emotions, I'll give them too much power.

That's why acknowledgment feels scary. We think, *How can clarity come from leaning into the chaos of my feelings?!* Carrie, a member of my email community, shared that her biggest struggle with navigating her feelings was this very issue—that they would cause her to plunge deeper into "woe is me" thinking. On the surface, acknowledging all the feels seems like it will land us in a perpetual pity party, which is the exact opposite of what we want.

Truth #1: We can accept what we're feeling without the emotions taking over or forever wallowing in the pain.

I didn't learn how to process emotions or understand that emotional expression was even permissible until later in life, so my emotions felt unfamiliar and uncontrollable. They were like volatile and unpredictable ticking time bombs inside, so my knee-jerk response was, *Yep, better leave those alone.* Sound familiar?

Three things helped me break free from the lie that if I leaned into painful emotions I'd never escape their vortex.

First, scientists have found that it takes ninety seconds, on average, for our brain and body to process a frustrating-in-the-moment emotion. After this initial processing we have the ability to decide whether we will wallow in the emotion and let it spiral out of control.[6] This truth has given me courage to begin practicing *acknowledge* because I know that a heightened emotion isn't going to last forever—I can handle ninety seconds—and I have the choice on how to handle the feeling moving forward.

When I need additional support not letting my acknowledgment spiral, I set a timer and allow myself to have a pity party for a certain amount of time, such as five minutes. When the timer goes off, I wipe away the tears and start the process of moving forward.

We can notice our emotions without getting stuck in them. Our bodies aren't designed for perpetual emotional agony, and our minds can rise above the turmoil and decide what we will focus on, like the air traffic controller example in chapter 3.

Second, it really helps to believe that God is with me in the emotion and won't abandon me when I am distraught. The Holy Spirit faithfully reminds me to consider logic when I've been emotionally wallowing. Plus, He keeps His promise to offer good ol'-fashioned conviction should I go off the rails in any aspect of life.

Third, I remember that *acknowledge* is just the first stop on this emotion-management train. In *discern*, we'll spend plenty of time looking at how to balance the volatility of our emotions with the grounding logic of biblical truth. We can't let ourselves get lost in the lie that *acknowledge* is the only filter we're using to examine the situation. *Acknowledge* and *discern* meld beautifully in step 3 of ADD, when we *decide* how to take Christ-centered action.

Let's not believe the lie that acknowledgment will add to the drama or keep us mired in unpleasant feelings. Let's notice what we're feeling, have a quick cry if we need to, remember God's presence, and stay open to the next steps of the ADD process.

Fear #2: "If I really focus on my emotions, I'll nurture a negative, complaining spirit."

I'm going to try to say this without sounding mean, but complainers really get on my nerves. Truly. My kids know that, for me, whining and moaning—I believe the Brits call it *grousing?*—is the shortest route from *sweet momma* to *surly mamba*. We've all read and reminded our children of verses like Philippians 2:14, which talk about the importance of not being known as a complainer. And let's not forget that underlying pressure we feel to be positive and grateful in all things, two perspectives that seem in direct opposition to honoring painful emotions.

Anyone else see why it makes sense that we're afraid acknowledgment will breed grumbling and griping instead of healing and hope?

Truth #2: We can lament the pain without complaining about it.

There's a big difference between lamenting and complaining. We can openly acknowledge pain within the framework of God's goodness (*lamenting*), or we can bitterly curse our situation as wrong and see our circumstances as pointless (*complaining*). The issue is whether or not we can process emotional pain while still believing in hope and possibility.

When we're upset, we want our grievances to be seen. We want someone else to notice the pain and say, "You're right, that's awful!" Maybe our spouse, our boss, or our kids won't hear it or recognize the injustice. But God gives us space in the *acknowledge* step to express our displeasure and to ask the tough "Why, God?" questions. He listens to our grievances.

We all have moments when we question God, feel hopeless, or wonder how in the world a situation could ever work out for our good like Romans 8:28 promises, and that's okay. After all, we *are* humans with limited insight and foresight. We can't be expected to see our omniscient God's resolution for our difficulty when we're stuck down here in the muck of zero visibility.

These are the moments when acknowledging our emotions *can* nurture a complaining spirit, and truthfully, we do need to watch out for them. Our words have power, both in the spiritual realm[7] and to create life or death in our bodies.[8] According to neuroscientist Dr. Andrew Newburg, "a single word has the power to influence the expression of genes that regulate physical and emotional stress."[9] Consider that God *spoke* the world into existence!

Every thought has the power to *reinforce* negative perspectives or to *restore* a Christ-centered perspective. This is why we are told to speak life over ourselves and our families. Our words, spoken and unspoken, greatly affect our ability to receive God's healing in times of despair and to successfully pursue His good plans for our futures.

The Israelites spent forty years taking a journey that could have taken eleven days because they were stuck in disobedience and grumbling (Deut. 1:2). God gave His people several opportunities to switch their thinking from grousing to gratitude—hello, food rained from the sky every morning—and from arguing to trusting in His plan.

Looking back, we can see that teaching a group of former slaves how to emotionally transition from forced obedience to freeing dependence on God was one of the purposes of that journey. However, if we're locked in thinking that God is not on our side, or if we allow hope to dissipate like mist in the desert heat, it's natural for bitterness and closed thinking to reign instead.

We have to ask, Will we stay in these moments of gut-wrenching acknowledgment? Will we believe the lie that this is the end of the road and that we are without hope? Like Jonah, will we curse God and long to die because things didn't work out the way we wanted? (Jon. 4:1–10). Like Naomi, will we tell others to call us Mara, Hebrew for *bitter*, because we've concluded that it's God's fault that life is hard (Ruth 1:20)? What we choose to do *after* lamenting is what matters most.

It's important to note that *acknowledge* isn't necessarily a two-second process of hastily admitting the pain in order to zip through emotional healing. This is especially true when the emotions we're processing are multilayered, affect our identity, trigger previous pain, or even cause us to question the meaning of life.

On *The Christian Mindset Coach* podcast, author and speaker Nancy Hicks shared about the excruciating journey of losing her twentysomething son to cancer. She bravely revealed what it was like to question everything, including why God hadn't answered her prayers for her son's healing. As painful as it was, she admitted that acknowledgment before God was an important part of her grieving process and of coming back to herself after this tragedy. She testified, "The extent to which you enter into your pain with God is the extent to which genuine life is released in you. They're equal in measure."[10]

God gives us space in our lamenting to be confused and overwhelmed by pain, and the amount of time in this window varies from person and situation. There comes a point in any grief journey, however, where God says, "You've cried many tears, and I've been there for all of them. Now I'm inviting you to a new stage of this pilgrimage. I'm inviting you to see even the tiniest glimmer of hope in this situation." That's when we get to decide if *acknowledge* will become lamenting or complaining.

Watch Out for the Inner Critic

The *acknowledge* step can also trigger your inner critic, an internal, judgmental voice that tries to limit or stop emotional processing in its tracks. Instead of Jesus's loving compassion that offers a safe space to acknowledge, the inner critic (sometimes called the inner mean girl) brings condemnation and emotional dismissal that can shroud our feelings.

The inner critic discards the validity of our emotions with thoughts like, *What you're feeling is not important or that big of a deal.*

This harsh voice shames us and convinces us to keep our emotions hidden: *You're being a baby about this. Suck it up and move on.* It wields our emotions as weapons, convincing us that messy feelings are further evidence of our flawed nature: *Yep, this just proves you will never have your act together.*

This inner saboteur judges us for imperfect emotional responses, especially when we're trying to confront toxic emotional patterns: *You're still triggered by this? Why haven't you figured this out yet?*

It persuades us that we're bad Christians for feeling anything other than positive emotions: *Philippians 4:8 says to focus on what's pure and lovely. A good Christian just focuses on these things.*[11]

It silences what we're feeling, even twisting Scripture to keep our feelings secret: *Doesn't God call you to be a peacemaker in*

Matthew 5:9? It's better to keep the peace than to say something that would cause tension in others.[12]

The inner critic can even attempt to use a false interpretation of gratitude to keep us quiet: *You have so many other good things in your life! Be more grateful and stop focusing on the negative.*

No matter what this malicious voice sounds like, we can't discover full emotional healing if we're stuck in these destructive dialogues. So how can we manage this self-critical voice?

Understand the inner critic's purpose. The inner critic is often the voice of the subconscious mind trying to keep us safe. She is that helicopter mom who is well-intentioned but potentially destructive in her attempts to protect us. While her voice can be harmful in its hyperactive nature, it is still an important part of the brain's ability to keep us from making poor choices, so we don't want to eliminate it. We can notice why she's there and react appropriately to heed her helpful guidance.

Listen to her fears and worries. One of the worst things we can do is dismiss her words. While it sounds absurd, acknowledging our emotions starts by also listening to what this inner mean girl has to say. God loves every part of us, even this inner critic's seemingly inane rants. He challenges us to find understanding and empathy for this voice: *How might the inner critic be a voice from our past? Or how might she be warning us of future hurt?* We don't have to accept what she says as truth, but we can listen and note why she's triggered.

Respond with God's loving compassion. Instead of yelling back, we can calm down the inner critic by loving her with a soothing balm of compassionate understanding. We can bring her to the foot of the cross and assure her of the protection and solace found in Christ. We can remind her that, yes, risk is always there, but God promises to walk with us through every season and to provide for our every need. We can say, with a genuine heart, "Thank you for being concerned. I see what you're saying here. However, God is my trustworthy Father, and I see how He's using these emotions to grow me closer to Him. He wants me to work through my feelings and not to hide from them. Therefore, I'm choosing to believe that it's safe to let Him help me process in a healthy way."

We can't fully eliminate the inner critic, nor do we want to. Remember, she is there to help keep us safe. We can speak to her with kindness, however. We can calm her down by offering the comfort she's ultimately seeking.

Acknowledge Mindset Tools

Looking for practical ways to acknowledge feelings? Give these acknowledge mindset tools a try. These can be used in a formal way, such as processing in a journal, or in an informal way, like internal reflection. Neuroscience has shown that writing down our feelings reduces the amygdala's stress response and activates the logical prefrontal region.[13] Some emotions may not require this level of processing, and obviously, we can't always stop to journal our emotions in the midst of a busy life. Elisabeth, a friend of mine and a mom of eight, told me, "I need to know how to handle my big emotions on the spot. What can I do in the moment when I'm angry and hurt but still need to be a calm mom?"

Whether or not we're blessed with a houseful of little people to manage, when we find ourselves triggered emotionally, we can take a deep breath—or lean on another form of emotional prep from chapter 4—and give ourselves space to gently acknowledge and empathize with our feelings.

Questions for Mindful Reflection

- What thoughts am I having right now?
- What am I feeling in this moment?
- Why does it make sense that I'm struggling with this thought or emotion right now?
- Based on my past or current circumstances, why might this situation be especially triggering?
- How can I give myself compassion and grace for thinking or feeling this way?
- As I sit quietly before God with this emotion, what words of empathy does He offer?

Declarative Statements

It can also be helpful to complete these statement prompts based on what the questions for mindful reflection revealed. These declarative statements offer a summarized anchor point where the mind can rest in and practice each step of ADD. The declarative statements from each step can be assembled into a single ADD statement to use as an overall summation of what's been *acknowledged*, *discerned*, and *decided* about how to manage the emotion (more on this in upcoming chapters). Here's both a condensed and an expanded template to use for the *acknowledge* step, depending on the situation and your personal preference:

> **Condensed:** "It makes sense that I'm feeling [X emotion] because of [Y situation]."
>
> **Expanded:** "[Y situation] happened, and it caused [X emotion]. This is understandable because of how [X emotion] is related to [state any core needs triggered] and [state any unmet expectations], and it triggers reminders of [state any past hurts and future fears]. God offers me compassion by reminding me that [state any Bible verses or truths that God may have revealed], and this makes me feel [state any resulting emotions]."

Emotional Decision Practices for Additional Insight

Need more help to get the thoughts flowing? Here are four more practices to acknowledge an emotion.

Morning pages. This daily mindset practice is a favorite of mine—and of many of my clients. I first heard about it in Julia Cameron's book *The Artist's Way*. Grab a journal and simply write three full pages of words. Write about anything and everything. Write your to-do list, your worries, a prayer to God—whatever is top of mind. Morning pages is not about sharing deep, dark secrets, unless that information comes out. The point is to get those mental gears turning by moving the thoughts out of your head and onto paper so that you can become more aware of what you're thinking and notice patterns.

Track your emotions via the Emotions Tracker. Understanding what we're feeling and what triggers those emotions isn't always easy to discover. Even if it's not natural for us to name the emotion we're feeling or what caused it, I believe that we can all grow in our emotional literacy and ability to understand ourselves. One of the best ways to get started is to track our thoughts and emotions for a week. Write these down in a journal or in the notetaking app on your phone or download the free "Emotions Tracker Exercise" at the end of the chapter. It includes prompts to help you record your emotions and discover emotional patterns.

Recognize God at work. In what ways has God shown up as a caring Father in your life? How do you see Him proving His compassionate character and unconditional love for you? It's so emotionally and spiritually nourishing to meditate on biblical truths that bring comfort, especially when we cite evidence of these truths at work in our personal stories. I've found that acknowledging current examples of God's fingerprints gives me courage to stop running from what I'm feeling and to ask for His help in processing difficult emotions.

Get additional perspective from others. If you need help acknowledging and understanding emotions, consider enlisting the help of a trained counselor or coach. Sometimes we need outside perspective to see what it sounds like to compassionately care for our emotions. It can also be helpful to hear others explain why it makes sense that you are feeling certain emotions.

Overall, if acknowledging emotions feels overwhelming or frightening, take it a little at a time. Start by simply saying "I'm feeling (X emotion)," such as "I'm feeling sad." When you're upset, notice how your body responds without criticizing that response. If you can't cultivate compassion for why the feelings are there, start by just admitting that they're present and that God is also with you in the messiness. Remember that the emotional prep tools from chapter 4 are there to help you transition into the parasympathetic state so you can acknowledge your feelings from a responsive instead of a reactive state.

Acknowledging emotions is a critical piece in emotional confidence. Once our feelings have been seen and heard, we're ready to

A Is for Acknowledge

ask God for clarity in understanding truth from lies. Next, we will move to discerning emotions within the light of God's wisdom.

CHAPTER QUESTIONS

1. On a scale of 1 to 10 (1 being incredibly easy and 10 being extremely difficult), how would you rate your ability to notice what you're feeling and to name the specific associated emotions?

2. Do you worry that acknowledging your feelings will give them "too much" power, thereby making your emotions feel more intense and possibly harder to control? Explain why.

3. Do you struggle with an inner critic? If so, how does your inner critic play a role in your ability to acknowledge your feelings with compassion and without judgment? What phrases does this inner mean girl use to keep you from honoring and processing your emotions?

4. As you practice acknowledging your emotions with compassion this week, what larger emotional patterns, such as perfectionism and people-pleasing, do you notice?

Testimonial

Before using the ADD tool, I didn't sit with my emotions at all. I wanted them to be fixed or solved, and I couldn't let the healing work at its own speed. Acknowledging my emotions with God beside me has taught me how to actively rest in His care and provision. Now I'm much more patient with the process of managing emotions. It's also much easier to hold the hard emotions with open hands instead of closed fists.

Stephanie, coaching client

105

QUESTION

What if I can't determine what I'm feeling emotionally?

ANSWER

We can't acknowledge emotions if we don't understand what we're feeling! This is extremely common. While knowing what's going on inside is naturally easier for some, I believe that with practice and intentionality, we can all grow in this area.

My client Tanya was looking for ways to feel less angry and anxious. In a coaching session we discovered that part of her frustration in managing an in-the-moment emotion came from her own difficulty in identifying the feeling itself. "It's never been easy for me to see what I'm feeling and name it," Tanya shared. "I was not only frustrated about the issue but also incredibly frustrated that I couldn't express what I was feeling."

Emotional prep tools like taking a deep breath and giving herself permission to lovingly calm the anger were extremely helpful stepping stones for Tanya to eventually acknowledge the deeper emotions. Tanya also found that morning pages were invaluable in releasing pent-up thoughts and allowing her to acknowledge what was inside without judgment. This type of journaling took the pressure off and gave her permission for the thoughts to simply flow. "I didn't have to have it all together and to have all the answers," she said, "and this gave me space to hear what was going on inside."

Don't forget to check out the free downloads for *Emotional Confidence*! There's a quiz, helpful exercises, and even audio and video tools to help you continue your journey in managing your emotions.

Go to AliciaMichelle.com/Emotional-Downloads to access these free resources.

7

D Is for Discern

Recently, I dreamed about the young man who I'd thought I would marry when I was in college. We haven't spoken in thirty years, but in the dream, he told me stories of all he'd experienced since we last met. My heart thrilled being there with him, and all my wonderings about what happened to him were no longer a mystery.

The dream ended with a friendly hug goodbye, and I woke up feeling satisfied.

But about an hour later, some tricky emotions set in. Curiosity invaded my tranquil thoughts and quickly morphed into an idea that *tried* to disguise itself as wisdom.

"Listen, you're not going to run away with this person," my emotions reasoned. "But you *could* do a quick online search and find out what really happened to him."

I wondered, *Are some of the things I dreamed about him actually true? It would be so satisfying to find out!*

That's when my logical brain and the Holy Spirit stepped in, reminding me of the boundary God had guided me to establish years ago around this situation. I heard the Holy Spirit remind me not to reawaken any dormant feelings by giving in to my emotional desires, even if they seemed innocent. "I ended that relationship for a reason," God said. "Instead, savor the truth that I've given you an even richer treasure in your husband of twenty-three years."

We've all felt justified in crossing certain boundary lines because our feelings convinced us we needed to, we deserved it, or we had no other choice. Feelings are significant and deserve to be heard, and that's why *acknowledge* is such an important step. But if we're not careful, our emotions can be used against us to distort reality and to excuse sinful actions, and that's never a good thing.

How do we know when our emotions are leading us to discover godly wisdom or when our emotions are a siren song pulling us toward wrong behaviors? *Discern*'s goal is to tap into God's ultimate truth—as found in Scripture and spoken by the Holy Spirit—as we process emotions in order to confidently identify any lies or distortions that steer us away from God.

What Is Discern and Why Is It Important?

Discern is about examining our emotions through the Holy Spirit's clarifying voice. In *discern*, we step outside of the situation and ask ourselves to view our emotions in light of God's wisdom. Once we've given ourselves the gift of compassion and recognized the plausibility of a situation or emotion in *acknowledge*, then we can ask in *discern*, How does this line up with truth?

Discern's main goal is to answer these two questions:

What is true and what is not true about this situation?
What would God say about how to handle this?

In *discern*, Scripture's timeless truths become our compass for navigating challenging emotions. Metaphorically speaking, *discern* allows us to sit in the middle of a room surrounded by all of a situation's messy components and, using biblical truth as our guide, decide which items to keep and which to toss.

Discernment is vital when managing emotions because, unlike God and biblical wisdom, feelings are not steadfast, true,

The ADD Flow

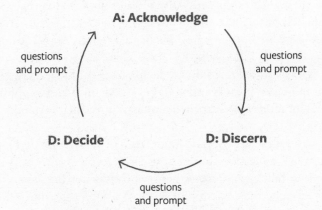

A: Acknowledge

questions and prompt

questions and prompt

D: Decide

D: Discern

questions and prompt

Acknowledge	Discern
Questions: • What thoughts and emotions am I experiencing? • Why does it make sense that I'm experiencing them?	**Questions:** • What is true and what is not true about this situation? • What would God say about how to handle this?
Prompt: "It makes sense that I'm feeling [X emotion] because of [Y situation]."	**Prompt:** "Yes, it's true that [state what is true]; however, it's not true that [state what isn't true]."
Caution: Watch out for the inner critic.	**Caution:** Watch out for mindset obstacles.

consistent, and trustworthy. Psalm 19:7–11 states that God's ways are perfect, and in contrast, human emotions are highly volatile and ever-changing, limited in their understanding and perspective, and representative of a given moment instead of a full picture. Our feelings are influenced by psychological needs, subconscious thought patterns, biological changes, environmental factors, distinct worldviews, others' opinions, the presence of our other feelings, and more!

While our emotions are valid and can be helpful, they can also cloak themselves with half-truths or outright lies that make them deceptively harmful. The Bible is filled with tragic stories of those who let their emotions be their guide: Cain's jealousy caused him to kill his brother Abel (Gen. 4:3–8); David's desire for Bathsheba led to adultery (2 Sam. 11:2–4); Judas's greed led him to betray Jesus (Mark 14:10–11); Ananias and Sapphira's thirst for money made them lie, which caused their instant death (Acts 5:1–11).

Without the appropriate boundaries of Holy Spirit–led logic, emotions can lead us into poor decisions with disastrous consequences. Like the difference between the comforting flames of a fireplace and the catastrophic torch of a forest fire, our feelings can be used for blessing or destruction. Clearly human emotions need the container of godly wisdom to stay in check.

This is why, as Christ followers, we cannot follow the world's advice to just "listen to our hearts" since human hearts can be deceitful and influenced by worldly concerns (Jer. 17:9). The Bible describes human knowledge as "partial" while God's knowledge is complete (1 Cor. 13:12 NLT), and we're called to trust in God's understanding of a situation instead of our own. Because we're called to take every thought captive to Christ, we must determine which voices in our head we will accept and reinforce and which we will lovingly surrender because they are unhelpful in our pursuit for holiness and Christ-centered living (2 Cor. 10:5). We must run every emotion through our truth filter—the Word of God—to seek wise direction through the heady fog of our emotions.

What Is God's Role in Discern?

As the ultimate authority of what's right and wrong in our world, God's wisdom is above human logic. As it says in Scripture, every one of God's words proves true, and His statutes stand forever (Prov. 30:5; Isa. 40:8). His truth convicts us to the core, judging even our heart's hidden beliefs and motives (Heb. 4:12). But how do we receive this holy discernment? Not only do we have the canon of Scripture as our guide but we've also been given the Holy Spirit Himself as a guide to remind us what Jesus taught us and to direct us to God's ultimate wisdom.

In light of these facts about the power of God's discernment, is anyone else intimidated at the thought of asking the supreme authority of the universe for help in sorting through our fallible emotions? Asking for a friend.

It's true that inviting this kind of intense exposé into our tender emotions would be terrifying if it wasn't balanced with the full truth about God's character. Yes, God has created everything we see, and Jesus will judge the living and the dead, but we also know our Lord as the kind and compassionate Savior who took on the world's burdens and who lovingly leads His sheep like an ewe with her lambs. We can stand on the promise that welcoming the truth into our emotions—even if that results in God's loving conviction—will set us free to make wise decisions that bring life to our bodies and praise to God.

Jesus gives the ultimate example of what it means to allow God's Word to shape our thoughts, emotions, and actions when He says, "I don't speak on my own authority. The Father who sent me has commanded me what to say and how to say it. And I know his commands lead to eternal life; so I say whatever my Father tells me to say" (John 12:49–50 NLT).

Let's dive into how godly discernment helps us practically manage emotions, especially in the heat of the moment.

God reveals limiting beliefs, preconceived notions, and other filters that distort our perspective. When we're in the depths of emotion, we're convinced that our hard times will never end, that we won't have the strength to go on, and that our problems will never be solved. In *discern*, God reveals how fear, hurt, past experiences, and even our own sin may be distorting our ability to see truth. Biblical wisdom in the midst of emotion can bring everything from corrective action, such as the case of the whining prophet Jonah inside a large whale, to comforting assurance, like when God comforted Hagar by reminding her that He would make a great nation from her son's descendants (Gen. 21:18).

God helps us link emotions to core needs and established patterns. Discernment provides opportunities for long-term transformation. As we grow in emotional confidence and notice behavioral patterns, we can seek the Holy Spirit's wisdom to discern the motivation behind the feelings by asking ourselves, *What is it that I am really longing for or needing right now? How might these emotions be check engine lights for core needs that aren't being met?* If we see toxic paradigms, we can consider how God might be using these situations to help us resolve this emotional pain in a healthier way.

God uses our painful situations and resulting emotions to help us see Him or others in a new light. We often think, *Why is God allowing me to walk through this pain? What's the lesson?* Inviting godly discernment into challenging emotions allows us to consider if God wants us to change faulty thinking about others or even about Him. Do we need to let go of a grudge so we can move forward in a relationship? Is He using this situation as an invitation to stop worrying so we can finally find peace around an issue? This may sound like tough love, but perhaps it's time to change our behavior and use this pain as an opportunity to respond differently.

God's truth inspires us with hope beyond the pain. Godly wisdom broadens our viewpoint, allowing us to view our emotions in greater context than what we can see from our limited vantage point. The Psalms offer many examples of how pondering God's faithfulness and His character can set the stage for fresh perspectives on difficult situations. This renewed outlook opens the door to uplifting emotions like hope and joy and refocuses our gaze on a heavenly mindset (2 Cor. 4:18).

God's discernment gives space for the logical mind to kick in. The logical prefrontal cortex is designed to counterbalance the hotheaded, fear-driven amygdala. Listening to biblical wisdom slows down our emotional reactions so that we can step out of the knee-jerk dictates of raging feelings and make decisions with a level head. We make room for godly clarity when we take a deep breath and pause to listen to the Holy Spirit.

Watch Out for Mindset Obstacles

Discerning truth takes a true partnership with God that comes from a vulnerable, submitted spirit. We must invite Him into our feelings—He will never force us to accept Him—and maintain a soft, teachable spirit that's willing to obey His words. If we're honest, that's easier said than done, especially when we're caught in emotion's heady grasp. Let's discuss three common ways even committed Christ followers block the power of discernment as they manage feelings.

Issue #1: Not Taking Care of Ourselves

Our lack of physical, emotional, and spiritual rest can definitely weaken our ability to hear God's voice (more on this in chapter 17). While it's hard to find scientific studies that directly link the connection between poor self-care and the ability to hear God's voice, we have all experienced how a lack of sleep, low blood sugar, or even inadequate hydration has affected our ability to think logically. (Being hangry is a real thing.) Hormonal changes, illness, or environmental factors can switch us into survival mode, thereby causing us to lean on emotion and away from higher-brain processing, such as spiritual discernment. Even social factors— like feeling well supported by a circle of friends and loved ones or feeling alone in our troubles—can affect our ability to hear God's wisdom when managing emotions.

In 1 Kings 19, the prophet Elijah flees into the wilderness after his life is threatened. Interestingly, Elijah had just experienced an intense outpouring of God's miracles in his ministry. Yet despite seeing God's presence in a mighty way—defeating hundreds of prophets of Baal with the power of God, to name just one—he prays for death as he falls asleep under a broom tree. The Lord meets Elijah's physical needs for water, food, and rest *before* He advises Elijah on his next steps. God decided that even this mighty prophet needed his physical needs met before he could absorb wisdom. God's voice is harder to hear when we're depleted, so self-care is important.

Issue #2: Not Listening to Truth When Emotions Are High

God's truth sets us free, but sometimes that wisdom can be more than inconvenient; it can be absolutely painful to obey. And if we aren't willing to follow God at all costs, what's the point in asking for wisdom? We must ask ourselves if we are willing to allow God to honestly examine the motives and intentions behind our emotions.

We'd love it if God's discernment simply confirmed our hot-blooded emotions as gospel truth, but submitting ourselves to God's authority means admitting we don't have all the answers, even if our feelings seem right in the moment. It takes spiritual maturity and trust in Christ to admit our feelings and be open to biblical advice. David offers a beautiful model in Psalm 139:23–24:

> Search me, O God, and know my heart;
> test me and know my anxious thoughts.
> Point out anything in me that offends you,
> and lead me along the path of everlasting life. (NLT)

This verse shows David's willingness to open his heart wide before God for insight. He admits that he has anxious thoughts, and he invites the Lord to advise him on how to align his feelings with his ultimate desire to trust and obey God.

Although David's open invitation to be searched by God is incredibly admirable, let's be real—it's also more than a little intimidating. *Point out anything in me that offends You, God?* It sounds great in theory, but like Jack Nicholson's famous quote from *A Few Good Men*, maybe you, like me, are thinking, *I "can't handle the truth!"* Knowledge comes with a responsibility to respond, and it can be scary to trust an unseen God with the tender places of our heart, especially if we are new in our faith or we've been hurt by others.

Remember the emotional iceberg from chapter 4? While anger, embarrassment, fear, and pride *can* be surface-level emotions, they can also hide below the surface and make it hard not only to discern God's voice but to obey His advice. As humans we naturally want to be right, and we want things our way. If we're not careful, we can interpret God's wisdom through these misleading filters as we look for God to give us the answers we *want*, not the answers we *need*.

Friend, we can only receive the blessing of discernment if we are willing to let God speak honestly to us. The world tries to convince us that truth is subjective and emotion is supreme. I don't mean to meddle in your business, but like a good mama bear, I need to ask, Are you willing to lay down your feelings before the whole truth of God and listen to what He says?

Once we're willing to listen, then we come to the second crossroads: Will we obey God when He says one thing and our flesh says another? We can't let anything, even reasonable, well-intended sentiment, override godly wisdom when it comes to discerning our feelings.

In the garden of Eden, Eve knew God's command not to eat the fruit of the tree of the knowledge of good and evil, but she allowed her emotions and human wisdom to supersede God's command. Eve's reasons for eating the fruit weren't based on bad desires. The tree was beautiful, the fruit looked delicious, and she wanted more wisdom—all good things, right? However, her emotional desires became sin when she decided to knowingly step outside of truth in order to get those things.

It's also important to note that God's voice becomes harder to hear the longer we're stuck in sin. Romans 1:18–28 speaks of the slow heart-hardening that happens when we ignore conviction and choose what feels right over what God says is true. Emotions like bitterness and anger can quickly manifest into catastrophic sin issues if we aren't willing to obey God's loving call to obedience.

On that note, it's critical that we keep our hearts emotionally pure before God so that we can tell the difference between the enemy's caustic voice of condemnation and God's healing voice of conviction. Check out the following chart for a quick comparison of conviction and condemnation.[1] We'll talk more about this topic in chapter 12.

Condemnation	Conviction
Rough, rude, hurtful	Tender, gracious, healing
Based on lies	Based on truth
Aggressive and cruel	Firm but kind
Points out faults	Lovingly draws attention to growth areas
Denies your identity as God's child	Affirms your identity as God's child
Rubs your nose in the sin	Champions your ability to change
Provides no hope for change	Provides a hope-filled way out
Tells you you're all alone	Offers to walk with you
Draws you away from God	Draws you closer to God

I'm sure I'm not the only one who has wondered how Judas could go from being a disciple and friend of Jesus to literally betraying Him to the Roman authorities. However, when we learn that Judas indulged in little temptations, like taking some of the disciples' money for himself, it's easy to see how Judas's heart became hardened to the point that he was only listening to his own emotions and justifications for greed. Instead of seeking God's will, the Bible says Judas began to look for a way to betray Jesus once he was tempted by the priests' offer.

If we want God's discernment to help us balance emotions, we first must have ears to listen and hearts willing to obey.

Issue #3: Allowing Our Definition of God's Truth to Shift or Become Distorted

Despite knowing Christ for years, most Christian women I work with hold on to some form of limiting beliefs, half-truths, or downright lies about themselves or God. These falsehoods are incredibly subtle, hidden under mountains of guilt. Often these committed Christ followers are surprised to discover how believing truth in their head but not in their heart has greatly affected their ability to find mental clarity and manage emotions well.

I liken this situation to having clogged air ducts in our homes. We don't notice the dusty, plugged-up ventilation shafts during the mild weather months. But when summer's heat strikes or winter's cold invades and the vents can't blow air because of the blockages, we suddenly see the problem and want it fixed immediately.

In the same way, many of us have slowly allowed our disappointments, mistakes, confusions, and hurts to block the Holy Spirit's voice in our emotional management, and we don't notice this blockage until we're smack-dab in the middle of intense pain. Upon examination we recognize that these wounds have spread across our relationship with God like a cancerous tumor, eroding our ability to trust Him or to allow His truth to be a guiding light when times are hard.

How can this happen, especially when we sincerely long to follow God?

First, to be fair, most of us have never learned how to balance our emotions with godly wisdom. As a result, many of us ignore, avoid, or push down our emotions, and these unprocessed emotions can quietly fester into distortions about God's goodness and love.

Second, the world's influence further confuses our truth-o-meter as we allow biblical wisdom to be only one of many filters for processing our feelings. According to research, daily Bible reading has sharply declined in recent years, and this means many of us have inadvertently allowed other sources of "wisdom" to invade our thinking because we aren't hearing God's voice through daily Bible study.[2] Galatians 5:16–17 encourages us to walk by the Spirit and spend time with God so that we will be less tempted to gratify the desires of the flesh. In later chapters we'll talk about how daily time in the Word is one of the best ways to continually hear God's discerning Spirit.

Third, some of us have listened to our critical inner voice for so long it's become extremely difficult to hear only God's voice instead of also perceiving inner distortions as real. As we persist in these patterns, we find it hard to discover godly discernment, especially in those moments when intense emotions noisily push their way to the forefront. It's easier to slip into what our minds want to tell us instead of what God's truth longs to reveal.

As a Christian mindset coach, I regularly see how a "blocked" or nonexistent discernment filter slowly contributes to the development of all kinds of limiting beliefs and toxic inner soundtracks, especially around self-worth. Tabitha, one of my clients, shared how it'd been hard to find calm for her raging emotions because she unknowingly adopted all sorts of false beliefs about herself. "I assumed lies about my identity because of what happened to me, and I let those thoughts reside in my mind without checking them against the Word."

Many of us ride that middle line with God, going through the motions while unsure if we can let God's truth dictate our emotional management because, despite what we say outwardly, we're not sure we can trust Him. Another one of my coaching clients Bryn expressed that she used to view God as "a trickster" because, in her mind, He sometimes showed up in the ways she expected and other times He didn't.[3]

This is where the concept of *radical acceptance* can bring tremendous emotional freedom. *Radical acceptance* is a phrase often used when a therapy client is encouraged to accept a situation as it is instead of ignoring, avoiding, or wishing things were different.[4]

We can radically accept that God's truth may be hard to hear sometimes and that it may not always make sense to our finite minds (Isa. 55:9). We can also radically accept that He is a trustworthy, kind Father who only has our best interests at heart, just like the Bible proclaims.

Imagine how this simple decision to trust and believe could transform our ability to hear and obey His voice! Think how much more we'd be willing to lean into God's discernment if we stopped wondering *if* God loves us and instead chose to view our circumstances through the lens of the Bible's promises that He one hundred percent *does*. What if we chose to recognize that our "Why, God?" questions are reasonable and that there will come a time to release the unknowns to Him so that we can rest in His divine authority?

I don't mean to insinuate that mending these challenging mental dialogues happens with a snap of the fingers. There may be painful—and understandable—reasons why we find it difficult to trust God, and these need compassionate exploration. However,

I believe that many of us could take great steps toward healing by simply deciding to stand on truth instead of questioning it.

Reading and meditating on God's Word is only half the battle in our spiritual growth. We must also regularly ask ourselves how our own versions of "truth" may be blocking our ability to hear God's voice.

Discern Mindset Tools

What are some tangible ways we can clarify our feelings with God's discernment? Here are some questions to prayerfully consider and possibly journal about:

Questions for Mindful Reflection

- What does God's Word say about what I'm feeling?
- What loving conviction might God be offering?
- What limiting beliefs or half-truths may I be using to process these thoughts?
- What deeper truths may God be trying to reveal in order to help me grow?
- If I'm finding it hard to hear God's voice in this area, have I been taking care of my emotional, spiritual, and physical needs?

Declarative Statements

Remember, the declarative statements from each step of ADD can be assembled into a single ADD statement to use as an overall summation of what's been *acknowledged*, *discerned*, and *decided* about how to manage the emotion. Here's both a condensed and an expanded template to use for the *discern* step, depending on the situation and your personal preference:

Condensed: "Yes, it's true that [state what is true]; however, it's not true that [state what isn't true]."

Expanded: "Yes, it's true that [state whatever truths were revealed about X emotion]; however, it's not true that [state whatever lies or half-truths were revealed]. The Bible also reminds me of other truths about my situation and life in general, such as [state any other wisdom received from God], and these truths help me feel [state the emotions these biblical truths bring, such as peace or courage]."

Emotional Decision Practices for Additional Insight

In addition, consider these practices to help tap into godly discernment.

Make it a habit to spend time in God's Word every day. It can't be overstated that connecting with God through Bible study and prayer is one of the best ways to seek godly discernment for our emotions. Discernment is much easier to access when our minds have regularly been marinating in God's Word. The more time we spend *listening* to God's voice, the better we are able to *hear* it and *obey* His truth instead of what "feels right" in the moment.

Use a concordance to find Bible verses to discern wisdom for specific emotions. Once you've acknowledged an emotion as real, ask God to direct you to specific verses that will help you better understand His perspective on what you're feeling. Try to boil the emotion down to key words around the feelings, such as *anger* or *bitterness*, so that you can search verses by those terms in an online concordance. Look up the words in various Bible versions, consider synonyms (*sad* could also be *tear* or *weep*) and search the root word instead of a derivative (*cry* instead of *crying*). Consider Bible characters who also may have struggled with these emotions. Again, this is where regular time in God's Word comes in handy. Write what you discover in a journal so you can easily reference it in the future. You'll find a list of Bible verses for specific emotions in part 3.

Listen for how God may speak outside of the Bible. Prayer and meditation can be wonderful avenues for quietly sitting before God and listening to His voice. What is God revealing through sermons, Christian podcasts, worship times, other wise believers, and additional situations where you hear His voice? What themes or patterns do you notice? How might these bring clarity, encouragement, or conviction around emotions you regularly struggle with? But keep in mind, if these insights are from God, they will never contradict biblical truth.

Pause, take a breath, and engage the parasympathetic nervous system. Try calming practices like the emotional prep tools from chapter 4 to keep the parasympathetic mind switched on. Kandace, a coaching client of mine, recently shared how the simple practice of taking a deep breath and pausing before responding to her teen's abrasive comments helped her tap into God's wisdom. "When I wait even thirty seconds before responding, then I am able to listen to God instead of leaning on my first inclination to be angry and control the situation."

Mirror discernment and clarity. Imagine that someone very close to you is experiencing the same emotion. What godly wisdom would you share with them about how they are feeling? What truths from God's Word and from their own life would you highlight for them? You can have this conversation aloud or write it down in a journal, as if this person were sharing their emotions with you and you were responding to them. Once you've had this imaginary dialogue, review what you shared and see how you could apply this to your own situation.

Journal a conversation between you and God about what you're feeling. In this spin on a journaling practice, find a quiet place where you can be still before God and listen. Write down a prayer about what you're feeling and then notice what the Holy Spirit says in response. I like to label these kind of journal conversations with God as if I'm writing the dialogue for two characters in a movie, using the initial G for God, and M for myself. For example, I write M and then write whatever is on my heart. Then, as I feel the Spirit speak, I write G and write down what I hear. I can't tell you how many times this practice has brought tremendous clarity to my emotions!

Be quick to repent and release sin. Sin keeps us locked in shame, hardens our heart, and makes it difficult to discern truth. Do your best to keep a clean record before God when you make a mistake. Even if it's been a while since you were honest with God about your sin, there's never a better time than the present to confess it all to Him. When we admit our transgressions, He promises to bring healing and to restore our fellowship with Him (Ps. 32:5). We never need to believe the lie that we are too far gone to come back to God. Like the father in Luke 15 lovingly welcomed the prodigal son at his return, Jesus promises to be standing with open arms when we repent.

Now that we've learned how to recognize our emotions and determine how they compare to God's reality, let's consider what it looks like to take courageous action in the presence of emotion- and Holy Spirit–led truth. We'll discover that together as we explore the final step of ADD, *decide*.

CHAPTER QUESTIONS

1. Have you experienced a time when your emotions tried to disguise themselves as "truth" like I shared in the chapter's opening story? What was that like? What made it so convincing?

2. On a scale of 1 to 10 (1 being incredibly easy and 10 being extremely difficult), how would you rate your ability to regularly hear God's voice of discernment regarding your emotions?

3. What are some hesitations you have in discerning truth, especially when your emotions are tender? What comforting or convicting truths from this chapter did you learn that will help you work through these barriers?

4. Do you struggle with a "clogged" discernment filter? If so, how might this have developed? For example, do you feel far from God as a result of sin or disappointment that something didn't work out a certain way?

5. What limiting beliefs and toxic inner soundtracks make it hard for you to hear God's Word and believe it? What next steps may God be calling you to take in order to find healing for these inner lies?

Testimonial

When we're presented with an emotional trigger and we don't have a tool like ADD, we instantly downshift into the way we've always handled things. Sweeping generalizations take over, and we numb ourselves through old ways of coping that aren't God-honoring.

But with a tool like ADD, we can hold emotional triggers at a distance and consider, Huh, I've thought this before, *then ask,* God, what do You say is true about this? *We can see the enemy's schemes for what they are and get massive clarity to take a different action.*

Alexa, coaching client

QUESTION

I have a hard time discerning God's voice. Any suggestions on other resources that can help me learn more about this practice?

ANSWER

Sure! Two of my favorite resources on this topic are from two of my favorite Christian authors. Priscilla Shirer's *Discerning the Voice of God: How to Recognize When God Speaks*, an in-depth Bible study, is one of the most helpful studies I've found on this topic. Likewise, Mark Batterson's *Whisper: How to Hear the Voice of God* is equally insightful as the author explains how God's voice can be heard as seven different "love languages" (Scripture, desires, doors, dreams, people, promptings, and pain). I often recommend both of these resources to clients as they're great resources to teach readers how to better tune in to how God speaks to us as believers.

Don't forget to check out the free downloads for *Emotional Confidence*! There's a quiz, helpful exercises, and even audio and video tools to help you continue your journey in managing your emotions.

Go to AliciaMichelle.com/Emotional-Downloads to access these free resources.

8

D Is for Decide

About six hundred years before Christ, three Israelite men were living as captives in Babylon and refusing to obey the wicked king Nebuchadnezzar's commands. These men—Shadrach, Meshach, and Abednego—decided they wouldn't bow to anyone but the Lord, and as a result they were thrown into a fiery furnace.

Shadrach, Meshach, and Abednego were mighty men of God who exhibited incredible faith, but they were still humans blessed with the same emotions as you and me. I wonder how they were able to respectfully serve the king for years without allowing their feelings about the law's unjustness to get the better of them. As they were being placed inside the furnace, were they struck with even the tiniest bit of fear knowing what was ahead, or were they 100 percent confident in their decision to trust God? Also, how did they feel as they walked around in the flames, first, realizing that they weren't on fire; and second, seeing another person in the fire with them—a person many believe to be the incarnate Christ (Dan. 1–3)?

The Bible isn't clear about whether these men were as cool as cucumbers or were wound up with wild emotions through this trial. We do know that, for any human, the decision to put one's life on the line comes with at least some form of emotional wrestling between feelings and truth.

That's the place we come to in the final step of ADD. Once we've seen our emotion as understandable (*acknowledge*) and recognized what's true and not true about what we're feeling (*discern*), there comes a moment where we ask, Now what do I do with all of this? Shadrach, Meshach, and Abednego made their decision to follow God at all costs despite the intense inner emotions they must have felt. Can we also honor God with our decisions, even in the presence of challenging emotions?

What Is Decide and Why Is It Important?

Decide is about asking God for His will on how to handle our emotions in light of truth. In this step we're asking Him for courage to do the right thing with our feelings, even when surrounding emotions may tempt us to lash out or shut down.

Will we trust in the Lord and respond in His way? Or will we trust in ourselves and do what we feel is right? Courage and surrender are a big part of the *decide* step because we need God's supernatural boldness to listen to His direction instead of responding to our emotional impulses.

Therefore, *decide*'s main goal is to answer these two questions:

What action does God want me to take?
Where will I emotionally dwell?

Decide is the resolution of how to balance all the feels within the realities of both biblical truth and a fallen world. Out of the entire ADD process, *decide* requires the greatest level of trust and partnership with God because it often requires faith beyond what we can see or feel in the moment.

Not only do we need God's direction in *decide* but we also need His help in managing the subsequent difficult emotions we

The ADD Flow

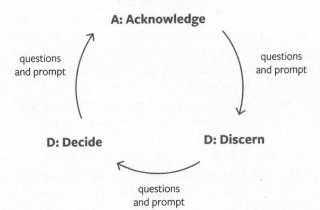

Acknowledge	Discern	Decide
Questions: • What thoughts and emotions am I experiencing? • Why does it make sense that I'm experiencing them?	**Questions:** • What is true and what is not true about this situation? • What would God say about how to handle this?	**Questions:** • What action does God want me to take? • Where will I emotionally dwell?
Prompt: "It makes sense that I'm feeling [X emotion] because of [Y situation]."	**Prompt:** "Yes, it's true that [state what is true]; however, it's not true that [state what isn't true]."	**Prompt:** "Based on what I've discovered, I'm going to [state the action], and I'm going to choose to emotionally dwell in [state the mindset you will focus on]."
Caution: Watch out for the inner critic.	**Caution:** Watch out for mindset obstacles.	**Caution:** Watch out for overthinking.

may feel as a result of this action. We want to not just outwardly obey God by making the decision but inwardly allow ourselves to release any fear attached to our choice, to refocus the mind on praising God, and to rest in quiet confidence. I call this *deciding where we will emotionally dwell*, and it's the critical other side of the coin when trusting God to help us know how to handle painful feelings.

What Is God's Role in Decide?

In the *decide* step, God helps us determine what to do with what we've learned about the emotion through the *acknowledge* and *discern* steps. He supplies us with courage and boldness to take the next step so that we can manage a specific emotional challenge well. He makes room for the imperfect by offering forgiveness and second chances should we flounder in our actions, and He also gives us the chance to surrender the difficulty of the unknown to Him.

What other ways does God work with us in the *decide* step?

God helps us discern which actions are our responsibility—and which are not—in order to resolve emotional tension. Because we are relational beings, we sometimes feel like our emotions are tied to the people around us. We'll talk more about managing emotions in relationships in chapter 16. For now, we can know that God helps us determine which aspects of a situation are ours to manage and which parts we need to release as someone else's responsibility. For example, *decide* might look like the choice to confess our part in a relationship conflict and to forgive the other person for their actions. Or the *decide* action could be allowing God to hold us in the midst of the emotional storm as He helps us surrender the reality of a situation that's out of our control. Note: If you need help remembering where your responsibility ends and begins in relationships, download the "Responsibility Proclamation" at the link at the end of this chapter.

God inspires us to take courageous action. Even with helpful tools like ADD, life's most challenging emotions are rarely resolved in neat, perfect packages. Sometimes we feel peace as we see how God wants us to bring resolution through the *decide* step, while other times we must challenge ourselves beyond our current faith level to decide if we will obey God's direction.

While trusting God in the messy middle can feel challenging, the bottom line is that obedience is an essential part of being a Christ follower. Demons know God as the supreme authority but refuse to obey Him unless God forces them to (Matt. 8:29–31; Mark 1:34; Acts 16:18). We can know God, but if we aren't willing to follow Him as our Lord, then—tough love here—our faith is no different from that of the demons. In the *decide* step, God graciously inspires us to boldly follow His lead, even when the choice is difficult.

God encourages us to release anything that distracts us from following His direction. In Hebrews 12:1 God calls us to run the race before us with perseverance, and that's hard to do when there is other physical, emotional, or spiritual baggage weighing us down. If following God in the *decide* step feels extra heavy, consider if the "check engine light" on this emotional situation is also a call for overall life change. Does He want to address other aspects of our past or current circumstances in order to resolve this emotion? Have we allowed for emotional or spiritual "clutter" in our connection with Him that makes it hard to trust Him? Take some time to prayerfully ask Him to reveal what, if anything, may be making this step especially challenging.

God equips us with strength and comforts our fears as we surrender the outcome to Him. The caring, compassionate God of *acknowledge* is still present in *decide*. He knows how challenging it can be to step out in courageous faith if you need additional time for full healing from an emotion. Surrendering the emotion itself can be a process! We may not be able to comprehend every aspect of the situation, and like David's example in Psalm 131:1, we can choose not to concern ourselves with matters that are beyond our understanding. Instead, David gives us this beautiful word picture in the next verse: "I have calmed and quieted myself, like a weaned child who no longer cries for its mother's milk" (v. 2 NLT). As we sit in the unknown, we can ask God for strength to calm and soothe our worries and, as a result, allow our mind to rest in hope-filled peace.

Are We Willing to Move When God Says Go?

God will not force us into action because love is patient and kind, and He is the incarnation of love itself (1 Cor. 13:4; 1 John 4:8). He guides us to a decision, but we must choose what we will do with the information.

At the pool of Bethsaida, Jesus asked a crippled man an interesting question: "Do you want to get well?" (John 5:6). We can say we want wholeness and emotional resolution, but are we willing to do what it takes to get it? Are we willing to quit our excuses, leave our pity parties—these warm, comfortable places—pick up our proverbial mats, and walk as Jesus challenged this man to do?

Earlier this year I met a cancer warrior named Melissa whose resilient faith and decision to follow God through the up-and-down emotions of her cancer journey rocked my world. She shared how God used this story of Jesus's encounter with the crippled man to break her from her own emotional turmoil about her diagnosis.

"I hate that I have cancer," Melissa said. "But God reminds me that He is with me in my sadness, pain, and grief. He tells me, 'Yes, this is your diagnosis, but no matter what's ahead, what will you do with your life? Daughter, it's time to stop wallowing. Pick up your mat and walk.'"[1]

Here's the ultimate *decide* question: Will we choose to allow the emotion to take over and fully dictate our response, or will we consider both the emotion and the truth together so we can take decided action toward God's plan for healing, even if that plan is uncomfortable? We must be *more* uncomfortable with living in the unresolved emotions than with stepping into the discomfort of following God's new way forward.

Trusting God in the Midst of Intense Emotions

As I type these words, I'm away for the weekend on a writing retreat, which is a glamorous way to say that I've locked myself in a hotel room for a few days with my laptop in order to meet my book-writing deadline. When I finished the previous chapter, I took an hour break to grab a quick bite. Even though I have a good outline for this chapter, I sometimes find that starting a new chapter triggers that inner voice that questions whether or not I'll be able to adequately gather my thoughts, and that's what's happened here.

I decided to take a few extra minutes to clear my head by walking around my favorite home decor store. While perusing the aisles

I found a framed quote that read "I trust the next chapter because I know the author." Isn't God funny? Seriously, you can't make this stuff up! It was a good reminder that I can trust Him to help me through every part of this writing process, even if my emotions try to convince me otherwise. I can recognize the doubt as reasonable but let His truth be my guide to keep me moving forward. I bought the frame, and it's now sitting across from me on the couch as I write.

Trust is an essential element of obedience. We can't lay our tender emotions before God and honestly follow His lead in the *decide* step if any trust issues are present. It's normal to sometimes struggle to connect with God or to understand His ways because it's hard for imperfect, finite humans to be in a close personal relationship with a perfect, infinite God. However, if we don't address these issues and mistrust builds instead, we may find it especially challenging to obey. We all need reminders that we can trust Him to provide everything we need as we step out in faith to follow His direction because we know Him and His character.

If God's calling us to new levels of trust through the *decide* step, can we recognize that He is at work, even if we don't see it or feel it yet? The biblical character Joseph was enslaved and in prison for years before he saw God faithfully bring emotional resolution to His family. We must train our eyes to see God at work, move forward in obedience, and hold on to His promises when the evidence hasn't quite made itself known yet. We don't need to see it to believe in it and to take action. This is the very essence of biblical faith.

Psst . . . does your heart still need something more concrete to move forward in managing your emotions well? After this chapter, I'll show you how to use ADD to write a tangible proclamation that includes all the parts you've been gathering through acknowledge, discern, and decide. You can focus on this ADD statement when this emotion reoccurs. Clients tell me that they love having these ADD statements because they really do remind them of what they've discovered and where they want to emotionally dwell.

Speaking of where we will emotionally dwell, let's consider this other important aspect of the *decide* step.

Choosing Where to Emotionally Dwell despite Our Frustrations and Fears

If we find ourselves struggling to feel content about trusting God with our emotional response, it's time to release, refocus, and rest. Philippians 4 offers a great model of this process.

Release Any Fear or Worry about the Decision

Do not be anxious about anything, but in every situation, by prayer and petition, with thanksgiving, present your requests to God. (v. 6)

Releasing (or surrendering) fear helps us more readily accept God's plan for emotional resolution. While surrendering fear of the unknown can feel challenging, we can find comfort in knowing that surrender doesn't mean giving *up* but giving *over*. It's not abandoning the issue or pretending like our feelings aren't important. Releasing fear is an active choice to redirect responsibility back to the person in charge of resolving the issue—God. To use a sailing analogy, we can do our best to adjust the sails, but God ultimately has to bring the wind to move the boat forward. Releasing our fears and worries is the ultimate act of trust and faith in action.

Refocus the Mind on Praise

Finally, brothers and sisters, whatever is true, whatever is noble, whatever is right, whatever is pure, whatever is lovely, whatever is admirable—if anything is excellent or praiseworthy—think about such things. (v. 8)

If we want to avoid going right back to whatever emotion we've been processing, we must give the mind something new to focus on. Surrendering unhelpful aspects of an emotion so we can move forward is like clearing away a patch of weeds in a garden. Yes, it results in a clean open space, but if we don't plant new seeds, the weeds will take over and grow again. Refocusing the mind on praise is the secret sauce in breaking free from what I call the worry-release-worry cycle that so many are stuck in. Lots of women tell me, "I tried releasing my worry to God, but it came right back!" That's because they didn't do the active work of replacing those worries by refocusing them on God's true, life-giving healthy reality. Don't miss this step!

What will you choose to focus on instead? This is where the mindset of praise reigns supreme. Even in the difficulty, what can we meditate on that's true, noble, right, pure, lovely, or admirable? Both the pain and the praise are equally true, but we get to decide which will dominate our thoughts.

Rest in Quiet Confidence

And the God of peace will be with you. (v. 9)

God encourages us to confidently dwell in His promises. As Moses stood with his back to the Red Sea and witnessed the Egyptian army advancing upon the newly freed Israelite people, he encouraged the people to stand with quiet confidence. When the people became hysterical at the sight of the Egyptians, Moses invited them to manage their fear by remaining calm and confidently believing that God would rescue them (Exod. 14:5–14).

Resting in quiet confidence is an active state that requires trust and obedience. It is not easy, but it allows us to stay surrendered to the *decide* action step instead of allowing emotion to take over.

Isaiah 30:15 offers similar insight and, as a woman who prefers to take charge instead of resting in God, I find this Scripture both extremely encouraging and convicting:

> This is what the Sovereign LORD,
>   the Holy One of Israel, says:
> "Only in returning to me
>   and resting in me will you be saved.
> In quietness and confidence is your strength.
>   But you would have none of it." (NLT)

Did you catch that? God wants to bring us emotional rest, but we are the ones who run from this gift. Instead of resting in quiet confidence, we convince ourselves that our quick remedies and

Types of Fear: *Pachad* and *Yirah*

The Old Testament uses the Hebrew words *pachad* and *yirah* to describe two different types of fear. *Strong's Concordance* describes *pachad* as "dread," "panic," or "disaster"[a] while it defines *yirah* as "awesome" or "reverence."[b] Both terms are used in the Old Testament to encourage a healthy reverence for our awesome Creator, such as Abraham's *yirah* fear of God seen in his willingness to sacrifice Isaac (Gen. 22:1–12) and Job's *pachad* fear of God's majesty and power (Job 13:11–12).

We can use *pachad* and *yirah* to better understand our own fears. *Pachad* fear often arises when we perceive a real or imagined threat to our physical safety, such as the rational concern of a car crash while driving in a snowstorm or an irrational worry that our children will be abducted. *Yirah* fear is the apprehension and awe of stepping into something bigger than our own capabilities, such as when we're called to launch a new endeavor or to trust God to provide during a time of unemployment.

How can we tell the difference between *pachad* and *yirah*? Both evoke a feeling of being outside of one's comfort zone, but in the book *Playing Big*, author Tara Mohr describes *pachad* as "lizard-brain fear" that feels like a physical contracting and restriction, and she describes *yirah* as "life-giving fear" that brings spaciousness and awe.[c]

We respond to *pachad* fear by employing the gift of wisdom to manage what's in our control and the power of godly surrender to release what's out of our control. We respond to *yirah* fear by pressing into the feeling and seeking God for strength to accomplish the mighty task ahead. We turn away from *pachad* and lean into *yirah*.

By examining fear through the lenses of *pachad* and *yirah*, we can turn toward God and our big emotions instead of turning away from them when the difficulties of life occur.

a. *Strong's Concordance*, s.v. "6343.pachad," Bible Hub, https://biblehub.com/hebrew/6343.htm.
b. *Strong's Concordance*, s.v. "3374.yirah," Bible Hub, https://biblehub.com/hebrew/3374.htm.
c. Tara Mohr, *Playing Big: Practical Wisdom for Women Who Want to Speak Up, Create, and Lead* (New York: Avery, 2015), 69–70.

instant solutions are better options. This is especially hard if we are box-checking, problem-solver people. Any fellow control freaks and perfectionists tracking with me?

Other biblical characters also used this concept of release, refocus, and rest to manage where they would emotionally dwell. In 2 Chronicles 20:1–24, Jehoshaphat was terrified when he heard that a vast army was approaching. He gathered the people together in Jerusalem and encouraged them to pray and fast. Once they praised God for His power, they were able to confidently release their fearful emotions and move forward. As a result, one of the men prophesied these words: "Do not be afraid! Don't be discouraged by this mighty army, for the battle is not yours, but God's. Tomorrow, march out against them . . . But you will not even need to fight. Take your positions; then stand still and watch the LORD's victory" (vv. 15–17).

Early the next morning as the army went out to the battle, Jehoshaphat reminded his men not to let fear take over but to emotionally dwell in God's promises and His power. True to God's Word, Jehoshaphat's men arrived at the scene ready to fight, but God had caused the enemy armies to fight among themselves so all the Israelites saw were dead bodies. Can you imagine how they must have praised God for His supernatural work? Talk about a faith-building moment!

We can trust God's leading and provision—even in the presence of our fears and heightened emotions—as we move forward in the *decide* step and choose to emotionally dwell in His peace. When we choose to release lingering pain, refocus fearful thoughts, and rest in quiet confidence, we make room for God's miracles, including our own spiritual growth.

Watch Out for Overthinking

Sometimes we get stuck in indecision because we need more time to process our emotion and to hear from God. This is a normal, legitimate response because managing emotions is a highly individual, often-messy experience with no hard-and-fast timetables.

However, indecision can be a cleverly disguised form of over-thinking, so we need to be on the lookout for this amygdala-driven freeze response. Overthinking, sometimes called *rumination*, can be the brain's last-ditch effort to keep us safe from perceived fears.

If we find our thoughts ruminating on all the what-if questions as we attempt to determine our best solution, we can ask ourselves if fear is present. Remember that, whether real or imagined, fear is the brain's way of keeping us safe. While fear is a reasonable human response to a possibly dangerous situation, it can also pro-long our emotional suffering and preclude us from making wise, godly decisions. We may know what God is calling us to do, but fear can convince us that the decision's unknown ramifications are more painful than continuing to slog through the emotional discomfort.

When we sense fear's presence, we can ask a few questions to untangle ourselves from its clutches:

- Why does it make sense that there's fear around this deci-sion? What's at stake?
- How is this fear attempting to protect me from getting hurt?
- What type of fear is present? Is it *pachad* fear or *yirah* fear?
- Now that I better understand why fear is present, how can I offer myself compassion for this fear?
- What's true and not true about this fear?
- What does this inner voice of fear need to know in order to find calm?
- How is God calling me to manage this fear in light of managing this emotion well? For example, do I need to surrender the unknown to Him? Do I need to avoid taking specific actions?

When we're stuck in overthinking as a result of fear, the only way to break free is to take action. This doesn't necessarily mean that we must immediately bulldoze our way to a decision without considering the attached emotions in a delicate situation. We can use the ADD process to manage overthinking as we take time to acknowledge the fear, seeing what's true and not true, in order to come to a reasonable conclusion for handling the overwhelming feeling. At some point, however, we must take action to counter the overthinking because action takes power away from fear.

One of my clients had a major breakthrough around this concept one day in a session. Shelby was terrified to move forward in a business decision because she'd been burned in the past and was afraid this decision would lead to failure. These fear-based emotions kept her paralyzed in a cycle of overthinking. When I challenged her to reconsider how she defined failure, she recognized that if she followed God she could not fail. Shelby saw that even if she didn't do it perfectly, God would, in her words, "slap some favor and grace on it" and she could keep moving forward. While her overthinking was a defense mechanism, she realized that this fear of failure had kept her in emotional turmoil and disobedience. Together we strategized ways to lovingly calm this inner voice of overwhelm so she could courageously follow God.

We must never let fear's false promise of safety lull us into inaction or even disobedience. We can choose to fix our eyes on the character of God, the example of Jesus, and the promise of the Holy Spirit's wise counsel to give us the courage to make decisions should overwhelm strike.

Decide Mindset Tools

Not sure what action God wants you to take in the *decide* step? If you have the luxury of time, spend some extra moments in prayer, Bible reading, or other spiritual disciplines like solitude, meditation, and fasting to seek His wisdom.

When we need to manage emotions in the moment, however, we can listen to the Holy Spirit's leading as a guide, which is why regular time spent soaking in God's Word is so important. As Psalm 37:30–31 promises, when God's law becomes our inner guide, we can be confident that we will not slip from His path.

Questions for Mindful Reflection

- What action is God calling me to take based on what He's revealed in the *acknowledge* and *discern* steps?
- How does this action step make sense in light of other things God has revealed about this emotion?
- What aspects of this emotion may I need to take responsibility for?
- What ramifications of this decision do I need to release because they are not my responsibility?
- If I'm hesitant to obey God by taking this step, what might be behind those feelings? How might fear and over-thinking be present?
- Where will I choose to emotionally dwell, especially if this decision is painful?

Declarative Statements

As we progress through the ADD steps, we can use these declarative statements as an overall summation of what's been *acknowledged*, *discerned*, and *decided* about how to manage the emotion. Here's both a condensed and an expanded template to use for the *decide* step, depending on the situation and your personal preference:

> **Condensed:** "Based on what I've discovered, I'm going to [state the action], and I'm going to choose to emotionally dwell in [state the mindset you will focus on]."
>
> **Expanded:** "Based on what I've discovered, I will take [state the specific actions you will take]. I will stand strong in the truth that [state any helpful truth revealed], and I will choose to believe God's promises for me, such as [state any other encouraging biblical truths]. I will continue to listen to God and offer myself compassion and grace as He leads me to healing and wholeness in this area."

In the wrestling for answers between logic and emotion, there's usually not a perfect resolution, especially if the *decide* step involves confronting risk or fear. It can feel excruciating to surrender an emotion to truth, to confess hidden sin, or to seek God's peace when we are obediently waiting for His resolution.

Emotional Decision Practices for Additional Insight

Try these action steps to help you as you *decide* where you will emotionally dwell.

Create a surrender board. Write down any fears or worries about this emotional decision on individual sticky notes. Read each note aloud, placing them on a piece of paper and surrendering them to God one by one. If you're stuck in overthinking, repeat something like "God, I trust that You've led me to a wise decision on how to handle this emotional situation. I am surrendering everything that is out of my control, and I'm trusting You to provide for every part of this situation."

Close the stress cycle. Even if the emotional stress has been relieved before the *decide* step, in many cases the body's biological fight-or-flight stress response remains engaged. In the book *Burnout: The Secret to Unlocking the Stress Cycle*, authors Emily and Amelia Nagoski state how we must "complete" the body's fight-or-flight stress cycle by taking physical action, such as strenuous exercise, to release the stress and signal to the body that it is safe to exit fight-or-flight.[2] Consider how a brisk walk, several minutes of deep breathing, or, yes, a few minutes alone for an ugly cry can help physically release the stress of working through the emotion so you can discover more peace in the *decide* step.

Keep talking to God about it. Whether it's formally written in a journal or communicated through prayer, ask God for help on how to emotionally dwell in a healthy mindset. If the *decide* step was especially painful, ask for God's help in keeping your thoughts focused on Him so you can rest in His perfect peace about the decision (Isa. 26:3).

Catch yourself in any overthinking or self-doubt that may come after the decision. If you find yourself questioning the decision over and over, lovingly acknowledge those thoughts, but don't allow yourself to become imprisoned in an inner inquisition. Check in with God to see if your concerns are from Him or if they are your own inner fears. Remind yourself that you've done your best to make a wise, God-honoring decision and you're always open to God's leading should He offer different insight. You can pray, *I'm not going to add unnecessary drama to the feelings by questioning myself over and over. Instead, God, I'm trusting You and dwelling in Your peace.*

Look for God sightings and regularly acknowledge how He's at work. Take time to notice His fingerprints throughout the day as part of a gratitude and recognition practice. When we're looking to dwell in emotional peace after a tough decision, it's helpful to remind ourselves that God is real, He's at work, and He cares about us in everyday situations.

CHAPTER QUESTIONS

1. Has God ever called you to obey Him in a decision that was painful or difficult? If so, what was that like? What did you learn about yourself and about God in that situation?

2. What real-world realities about yourself or other people might God want you to accept in order to wisely manage what you're feeling about a certain situation?

3. Is it hard for you to emotionally dwell in God's peace while wrestling with tough emotions? What Bible verses, stories, or other spiritual truths can you cling to in order to let go of what's out of your control and rest in God's promises?

4. How has fear played a role in how you manage your emotions? How did this chapter's insights on the connection between fear and overthinking bring new insights into how you can lovingly release yourself from rumination?

Testimonial

One of my biggest challenges is that I want to "cure" my emotions so that they are always positive. Before I had a tool like ADD, I managed unpleasant feelings by "doing more"—more exercise, more work, and more cleaning.

But ADD has helped me grant myself much more compassion for the not-always-positive thoughts I have. With ADD I can process toxic thoughts that try to creep in so that I can release them to God. This simple tool allows me to experience more times of peace and joy, and I use it at least once a day.

Sandy, coaching client

QUESTION

What if I've gone through all the steps of ADD and God's direction is still not clear?

ANSWER

Sometimes it's fairly easy to see God's leading and to know how He'd want us to emotionally respond. And other times God's answers to the *decide* step feel as clear as the murky waters of a moss-covered swamp. We are an instant-answer society, and we get a bit cranky when God's best decision for our situation doesn't materialize in our time frame. We crave control and sure bets, which means that we want God to deliver His perfect outline for managing our emotional chaos to our bedside while we sleep.

But that's not how God directs His people. He is not our trained lapdog that rolls over and barks at our command. There's a mystery to His ways, and sometimes He doesn't share the whole picture with us (1 Cor. 13:9). We have to be okay with that.

What we can do, however, is take the next best step based on what we've discovered after *acknowledge* and *discern*. Maybe we don't have the full picture, but based on what we know about ourselves, about the situation, and about God, we can ask, What is a

141

possible response? If we're still not sure, we can wait for God to show us.

ADD is often an intertwined process as one emotion influences another. As we acknowledge other, related emotions and seek discernment, the big picture pieces of the puzzle start to come together. We can keep asking God to speak to us through all the facets of ADD—the compassion of *acknowledgment*, the clarity of *discernment*, and the courage of *decision*. Sometimes the journey isn't linear, and this is especially true for complex emotions and ongoing situations. In the midst of all the facets of emotion, we can leave room for the unknowns and stay curious before God.

Don't forget to check out the free downloads for *Emotional Confidence*! There's a quiz, helpful exercises, and even audio and video tools to help you continue your journey in managing your emotions.

Go to AliciaMichelle.com/Emotional-Downloads to access these free resources.

How to Write an ADD Statement

Now that we've had a chance to examine each part of ADD in detail, let's talk about how to gather up what we've discovered so that we can create what we'll call an ADD statement to help us manage any persistent emotions.

Many women I coach consider an ADD statement an invaluable tool for managing emotions. In fact, many of them print out these statements and meditate on them regularly as they're working through an ongoing emotional situation.

As you'll notice, an ADD statement is the summation of the declarative statements we wrote for each step of ADD. Therefore, to create an ADD statement, gather up the individual declarative statement prompts from the *acknowledge, discern,* and *decide* steps. For your reference, here are the individual prompts from each step. Keep in mind that these are the condensed versions of the ADD statements (access the expanded versions on the "ADD Statement Worksheet" found at the link at the end of the chapter).

Acknowledge: "It makes sense that I'm feeling [X emotion] because of [Y situation]."

Discern: "Yes, it's true that [state what is true]; however, it's not true that [state what isn't true]."

Decide: "Based on what I've discovered, I'm going [state the action], and I'm going to choose to emotionally dwell in [state the mindset you will focus on]."

Here are three examples of how an ADD statement might sound using these condensed prompts:

Acknowledge: It makes sense that lately I've been feeling unsure if I should leave my job because I no longer feel challenged. I've been very emotionally drained, and this is why.

Discern: Yes, it's true that my career skills have greatly expanded while working here; however, it seems like both my earning and learning potential have reached their limit. I also know that I can't stay in a job long term when I'm not being challenged or if I'm not passionate about the company's mission.

Decide: Based on what I've discovered, I will start looking around for a new position because it will help me battle the daily emotional grind if I know that I'm not stuck in my present job forever. I'll also make room in my schedule for replenishing activities to counteract my exhaustion. I will choose to emotionally dwell in the truth that God will guide my job search, and as long as I am at this company, I will look to Him for emotional strength to serve my customers with excellence.

Acknowledge: It makes sense that I am worried and concerned about my mom. My aunt died of breast cancer a few years ago, and my mom just found a lump in her breast. The doctors want to do a more detailed ultrasound, and she asked me to come with her to the appointment. I want to be strong for her, but I can't deny my fear.

Discern: It's true that my fear is reasonable: yes, this could be cancer. It's also true that we don't know what's going on until the doctors do more testing. No conclusions have been determined.

Decide: I am in charge of whether or not this fear takes over my reality. It is reasonable, but with God's help, I can put fear aside and focus solely on what's been revealed so far. I can trust God with the outcome, no matter what it is. I can live in this moment and take it one step at a time.

Acknowledge: It makes sense I am frustrated by and worried about my teenage daughter because she has been completely unprepared for school lately. For the second day in a row, she has asked me to pick her up early because of headaches caused by her skipping breakfast.

Discern: It's true that I need to offer her grace because she's still a child who is learning to take care of her physical needs. It's also true that she needs to learn how to plan for herself and be self-sufficient.

Decide: Therefore, I will pick her up early today, but I will remind her of the importance of eating a nutritious breakfast so she can be strong for school. I will also remind her that she needs to own this responsibility. If this happens in the future, I won't pick her up early, and I will not allow myself to feel guilty about it.

Now you give it a try! Download and print out the free exercise "ADD Statement Worksheet" to create a statement for your situation. Remember, these are just templates. Feel free to express these concepts in your own words!

QUESTION

How long should my ADD statement be?

ANSWER

Wondering whether to use the condensed or the expanded version of the prompts? The length of your ADD statement depends on three factors: (1) the emotion itself, (2) the situation you're processing, and (3) your personal preference. You may find yourself with more to say than someone else simply due to the situation's emotional intensity or because you're a naturally wordy person with more to express. Or maybe it's the opposite. Conciseness is fine too. Sometimes clients start with a longer affirmation and then condense as the new thoughts become more comfortable.

Your confidence in how much or how little you personally include in your ADD statement will grow as you grow more comfortable with the ADD process. If you feel stuck and need inspiration, review the discovery questions and mindset tools for each step of ADD in chapters 6, 7, and 8 and check out the samples on the following pages.

Need more help in applying ADD to everyday situations? In part 3 we'll work through how to process six common emotions using ADD, including specific questions, Bible verses, and sample ADD statements.

Don't forget to check out the free downloads for *Emotional Confidence*! There's a quiz, helpful exercises, and even audio and video tools to help you continue your journey in managing your emotions.

Go to AliciaMichelle.com/Emotional-Downloads to access these free resources.

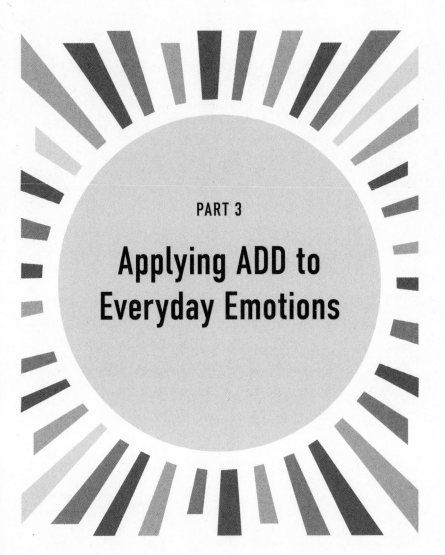

PART 3

Applying ADD to Everyday Emotions

How to Use This Section

If parts 1 and 2 are the classroom teaching behind the ADD process, part 3 is the laboratory where we experiment with these tools by applying them to six difficult emotions we face: anger, disappointment, worry, shame, discontentment, and loneliness.

Here's an overview of the sections in each chapter of part 3:

Introduction: This section provides a general explanation of what it's like to feel this emotion and how past hurts, core needs, and future fears can trigger it.

Questions for Discovery: This is a list of questions (divided into three parts) to use as a guide through the ADD system. Since these questions broadly relate to the emotion, choose questions that most resonate with you.

ADD Statement: Here's where you'll combine each of the declarative statements into a single ADD statement that expresses where you will emotionally dwell. This statement, which I sometimes call an *ADD affirmation*, can be repeated daily or whenever you feel triggered by a situation and its related emotions. By the way, this affirmation is flexible, meaning it can be modified as the situation evolves or as God reveals additional information to you. Let the Lord lead you in the moment as you process, realizing that there's no need to seek the "perfect" affirmation. Note: Download the free "ADD Statement Worksheet" from the link at the end of each chapter.

More Important Reminders

Remember what you've learned so far about managing emotions. Use supplementary processing tools, like emotional prep, to bring calm to heightened emotions in the moment. If emotions feel too intense to process using the ADD steps, try calming your mind and body to turn on the parasympathetic's "rest and digest" state so you can access your logical mind. It's extremely important to write down your thoughts as you process instead of keeping them in your head, especially when you first start using ADD. In addition, don't forget that feelings can show up as surface-level ("above the surface") emotions or as secondary ("below the surface") emotions. Process the emotion rising to the top first and then address any underlying emotions.

The Scripture lists are a starting point for biblical wisdom. The Bible verses included in each chapter are not meant to represent every verse on the topic but are simply jumping-off points for your discovery. Let God lead as you explore the verses and listen to the Holy Spirit for specific insight. To dig into the verses further, consider using a Bible concordance to look up synonyms and antonyms that relate to the emotion or try reading the suggested Scriptures in different Bible translations.

These prompts are guideposts, not boxes to check. Think of all the questions, Bible verses, and tools in these sections as a buffet. Do yourself a favor and release the need to answer every question, read every Bible verse, or use every emotion-processing tool. There are no brownie points for checking all the boxes. Perfectionists and overthinkers, I'm talking to you here.

Seek help from a mental health professional if needed. As I mentioned at the beginning of this book, any time we touch on emotional topics there's a chance that past or present emotional wounds could be triggered. ADD is a powerful tool for processing emotions, but you are responsible for your own mental health, including determining if you should enlist the help of a mental health professional.

Enjoy the journey and let God lead your timeline. You may be able to work through ADD in under a minute, or it may take much longer. If you've been working through an emotional issue for a while, you may have to spend more time in one part of ADD than another. As you become more familiar with the ADD process, you will naturally find yourself becoming more efficient. You may find that a question in one part of the process triggers a question in another part, and that's all right too. The method is often a circular flow instead of a straight line, and the goal is to get more clarity and insight as you process.

Most of all, relax and let the Lord lead you on this journey.

9

Anger

Anger is one of the most basic human emotions, and it is our mind, body, and spirit's first line of defense telling us that something is awry. Whether we feel jilted, hurt, or filled with rage, angry feelings can be an indicator or a natural consequence of frustration. That's why our goal isn't to negate or ignore angry emotions but instead to manage them in a way that honors God and protects our relationships.

First of all, is anger a sin? Although the Bible says that "human anger does not produce the righteousness God desires" (James 1:20 NLT), anger becomes sin when we act on the emotion in a way that goes against God's Word or hurts others. Ephesians 4:26–27 says, "don't sin by letting anger control you," and it reminds us that anger "gives a foothold to the devil" (NLT). If anger itself was a sin, then wouldn't the Bible directly tell us not to get angry at all? Some may argue that Ephesians 4:31–32 does state that we are to get rid of anger. However, when considering the passage as a whole, Paul is not admonishing the Ephesians for *having* anger but advising them on how to handle anger appropriately by allowing the Holy Spirit to renew their angry thoughts.[1]

In addition, the Bible states how both God the Father and Jesus experienced anger as a result of people's disobedience, sin, or injustice, which scholars sometimes call God's "righteous anger" (Num. 25:3; Deut. 11:13–17; John 11:33). God cannot be just if He does not allow room for the ability to express displeasure when His laws are broken or when horrific injustices take place. God promises to pour out His anger on those who oppose His people or who choose to rebel against His truth (Rom. 1:18). At the same time, the Lord describes Himself as "slow to anger, abounding in love" and often holds back His anger (Exod. 34:6; Isa. 48:9). By definition, a holy God can experience only a holy version of any emotion, which further proves that anger itself is not a sin but that it's the behavior resulting from anger that can lead to sin.

Anger can grow from displeasure, to annoyance, to irritation, to bitterness, to exasperation, to hostility, and eventually to rage. While every anger manifestation is unique, it's undeniable that anger's intensity becomes harder to manage the longer we allow it to build. Emotions build upon each other in the brain, and when anger is not regularly processed, the brain can short-circuit the earlier stages of anger, such as displeasure, and immediately go to more destructive versions, such as hostility. This all confirms the command in Ephesians 4:26 that we deal with any anger quickly so that it has less chance to manifest into sin.

Since anger can be such a potentially destructive emotion that can flare up in an instant, it's important that we have tried-and-true calming strategies at the ready—like the emotional prep tools in chapter 4—to kick on the parasympathetic nervous system when anger strikes.

Since we don't want to store anger in our minds and bodies, we need to express the intense emotion in safe ways. This can include praying, journaling, crying, or even moving the energy through the body via intense exercise. Anger puts the brain in fight-or-flight mode, so walking away from the situation that sparked the emotion to find space and solitude are also critical elements for anger management.

It can also be helpful to determine if the anger is coming from a reoccurring frustration, such as marital tension around a particular issue, or if it's anger without any deeper meaning, such as when someone cuts us off in traffic. When we notice anger from an ongoing issue, we can ask ourselves whether or not the feeling is present because a core emotional need—such as being loved and seen—feels threatened. If you notice that your anger stems from unresolved trauma, or if you suspect you may struggle with other mental health conditions, such as PTSD, it's wise to consult a medical professional.

Questions for Discovery

Acknowledge

- What specific thoughts of anger are you experiencing?
- To whom (or about what situation) is the anger directed?
- What other words would you use to describe the intensity of your anger (e.g., displeasure, annoyance, irritation, bitterness, exasperation, hostility, or rage)?
- How might the anger relate to not having your core needs met, such as a need for belonging or acceptance?
- Is your anger a surface-level emotion or a secondary emotion? If it's a secondary emotion, what other emotions may be present?
- After examining the evidence, why does it make sense that you're angry? Consider the compassionate words you'd share with a loved one who was feeling this type of anger, then speak them over your situation.
- Although God will not justify sin committed in anger, how might He comfort you with His understanding about why you are angry? Consider specific Bible verses, Bible stories, and examples from your past that show His care for you.

Create a brief statement about what you discovered in *acknowledge* (see page 103 for an example).

Discern

- How might a lack of self-care be heightening the intensity of your anger? Ask yourself the following questions:
  - ▸ Have I eaten something nutritious lately?
  - ▸ Have I had enough water today?
  - ▸ Have I moved my body recently?
  - ▸ Have I been getting enough sleep?
  - ▸ Do I have other complex or frustrating emotions inside me that need to be processed?
  - ▸ How might environmental or hormonal changes be contributing to the intensity?
- What filters may you be using to process your anger? For example:
  - ▸ Are you using black-and-white thinking to process the anger?
  - ▸ Is your anger causing you to believe lies or half-truths about the situation?
  - ▸ Is your anger based on an unknown, such as a fear you will be hurt by others or that this situation will never get better?
  - ▸ How might the fighter, runner, freezer, or pleaser personas be present as you're processing?
  - ▸ How might anger's threat to core needs impact how you're processing the truth of this situation?
  - ▸ Based on what you discovered, why does it make sense that you may be using these filters to process the anger?
- If the anger is directed at a person, is the other person's point of view understandable? Take a moment to think about why they may be in opposition to you. While your anger may still be justified, how does understanding their side of the story help you release your anger?
- How do Bible verses on anger (like Prov. 14:29; 15:1; 29:11; Rom. 12:19; Gal. 5:19–21; James 1:19–21) help you better manage your feelings?

- What deeper truths may God be trying to reveal to help you grow?
- What loving conviction might God be offering?
- What emotions do you feel after seeing God's truth about the situation?

Create a brief statement about what you discovered in *discern* (see page 119 for an example).

Decide

- How have your own decisions contributed to the anger, and as a result, what needs to be confessed to God or others?
- Which part of this situation is out of your control? How can you release this to God?
- If there are other people involved in this situation, is God calling you to speak to them about what you're feeling or is He encouraging you to process and release the hurt just to Him?
- What self-care rituals can you practice right now to help yourself work through the anger?
- Do you sense the presence of *pachad* fear or *yirah* fear (see chap. 8)? If so, how might God want you to handle this fear?
- What other spiritually centered activities, like prayer and worship, can you practice to surround yourself with God's loving presence in order to be released from the anger?
- How may God be calling you to rest in His ability to work all things out for your good in this situation?
- Where will you decide to emotionally dwell? Of what biblical truths will you remind yourself?

Create a brief statement about what you discovered in *decide* (see page 138 for an example).

ADD Statement

Combine each of the statements from the ADD sections into a single affirmation. Here's an example in both condensed and expanded form:

Condensed Version

Acknowledge: "It makes sense that I'm angry because my husband was rude to me about not wanting to go on a double date this weekend. It's been a hard week, and I was really looking forward to getting out of the house together and doing something fun with friends!"

Discern: "Yes, it's true that his comments hurt me, but I see that he wasn't angry at me. He is exhausted from being gone and just wants to stay home and rest. I also see that I am more sensitive right now because I, too, am exhausted from taking care of the kids. It feels like this travel season will last forever, but I know that's not true."

Decide: "In light of this, I'm going to forgive him for what he said because I know it wasn't meant to be hurtful. I will do my part to help us grow closer together by working on ways for both of us to get our different rest needs met. I'm also going to make a point to spend extra time with God so that I can stay focused on the truth that He is with me in all situations and that our family will make it through this."

Expanded Version

Acknowledge: "My husband was incredibly rude to me tonight so it makes sense that I'm angry. He's been traveling all week, and I was looking forward to spending quality time with him so I was crushed when he snapped at me about not wanting to go out with our friends. I'd been planning this double date in my mind all week, and I was very excited to get out of the house, have a babysitter, and enjoy time together. I've been feeling neglected lately and like my needs don't matter, so his rejection was especially hurtful."

Discern: "Yes, it's true that his comments were short and hard to hear; however, it's not true that he doesn't want to spend time with me or that he doesn't love me. He is extremely exhausted right now from this extra travel, and as an introvert, all he wants to do is stay at home on the weekends to recover. I can understand that. I also understand that I'm worn-out from pulling double duty as a parent when he travels, and that makes me particularly edgy. It was a perfect storm of events—his being worn-out and wanting to stay home, and me feeling cooped up and wanting to get out. The good news is that this extra travel won't go on forever. Things will be challenging, but I know we can get through this."

Decide: "I'm choosing to let go of his hurtful comments. They were a reflection of his stress and not of his lack of desire to spend time together. I will not let the enemy use this to cause a wedge between us. I want to do my part to help both of us maintain our strength during this intense travel season, so later tonight, after the kids are in bed, I will share my heart with him about how I understand we're both tired and need to find ways to get rest. I'll also explore other ways that I can get help with childcare while he's gone—babysitting swap? help from my sister?—so that I can meet my need to get out of the house and be social with friends. This will help me not feel so desperate for downtime when he is home. I also know that I need some extra reminders from God that I'm not alone in this, so I will spend more time in my Bible and in prayer. This will help me stay centered on His truth so I can respond with love and grace."

10

Disappointment

Vulnerability—before others, before God, and before ourselves—is perhaps the riskiest of human emotions because it requires our soul to be laid bare and exposed to potential suffering. Many of us spend our lives constructing all sorts of facades, barriers, and distractions to avoid being burned by vulnerability. And this is why disappointment—and the related emotions of sadness and sorrow—are so painful. These emotions represent the distress caused when vulnerability is risked and lost.

Disappointment occurs when we get emotionally injured in our pursuit of something we've been seeking. We risk disappointment every time we open our heart to love, joy, and hope. And in a fallen world, the potential for disappointment is everywhere. Disappointment, sadness, and sorrow can stem from unmet expectations, unexpected hurt from others, or even frustration from our own inability to change.

Disappointment walks hand in hand with grief as it carries the weight of bankrupt hopes and unfulfilled dreams. As Queen Elizabeth shared with bereaved families of the victims of the 9/11 attacks and then again at the funeral of her beloved husband Prince Philip, "Grief is the price we pay for love."[1]

Disappointment is often a place of confusion as well as grief. It leaves us wondering, *Why didn't things work out the way I'd hoped? Why didn't God intervene and change how this story ended? Now what am I supposed to do with these broken pieces and tender emotions left in disappointment's wake?* Depending on the gravity and magnitude of the circumstance, disappointment can shatter hope itself and send us straight into despair.

This emotion is proof that we are creatures from another world who are ultimately created for heaven's perfection, where no tears are shed and where every desire is perfectly met. While disappointment may be part of this world, in Christ we have the ability to process it without losing our ultimate hope. By His power, we can notice the sting of lost vulnerability without allowing past disappointment to derail our future ability to trust.

The *acknowledge* step is especially important when navigating disappointment because acknowledgment leads to empathy—a sorely needed gift when disenchantments happen. We must build up our reserves of feeling heard and understood before we can risk confronting truth and asking the essential why questions (in the *discern* step). This is why it makes sense that we may linger longer in the *acknowledge* step—and possibly bounce back and forth between *acknowledge* and *discern*—as we work through disappointment.

We can give ourselves loads of grace to notice how this emotion awakens related hurts and fears and allow the reassuring, loving arms of God to help us reconcile our anguish with His purifying truth. We must do this deeper processing to honestly arrive at *decide* so we can comfortably risk planting new seeds of hope and choose vulnerability again in our own timing.

Note that if disappointment is the result of our sinful choices, then the Bible says that this type of godly sorrow, also called *conviction*, can be helpful because it "leads us away from sin and results in salvation." The apostle Paul tells us that there's "no regret" for this kind of sorrow (2 Cor. 7:10 NLT). We'll talk more about conviction in chapter 12.

Questions for Discovery

Acknowledge

- What specific thoughts of disappointment are you experiencing?
- To whom (or about what situation) is the disappointment directed?
- What other past disappointments, hurts, or fears does this disappointment trigger?
- How might the disappointment relate to not having your core needs met, such as a need for belonging or security?
- Is your disappointment a surface-level emotion or a secondary emotion? If it's a secondary emotion, what other emotions may be present?
- After examining the evidence, why does it make sense that you're disappointed? Consider the compassionate words you'd share with a loved one who was feeling this type of disappointment, then speak them over your situation.
- What comforting words would God offer? Imagine how His comfort might translate into physical forms such as envisioning His compassion as a big hug; His loving care as a gentle rain shower; or His comforting presence sitting beside you as you process.
- How do you feel after acknowledging the disappointment as real and receiving godly compassion?

Create a brief statement about what you discovered in *acknowledge* (see page 103 for an example).

Discern

- What filters may you be using to process your disappointment? For example:
  - ► Are you using black-and-white thinking to process the disappointment?

162

> ► Are related emotions like anger and grief causing you to believe lies or half-truths about the situation?

> ► Are you believing the lie that you will be stuck in disappointment forever and things won't change?

> ► Are you allowing fear and pain to assume future outcomes and to ignore the wild card of how God may solve the issue outside your understanding?

> ► How might the fighter, runner, freezer, or pleaser personas be present as you're processing?

> ► How might disappointment's threat to core needs impact how you're processing the truth of this situation?

> ► Based on what you discovered, why does it make sense that you may be using these filters to process the disappointment?

- What does God say about mourning and disappointment (see Ps. 42:11; Isa. 61:3; John 16:33)?

- Consider where God is when you are feeling misunderstood, confused, and hurting (see Ps. 16:8; 23:4–6; 71:6).

- Think about where the Bible says your unshakable hope is found and what your response is to this hope (see Ps. 62:5; 78:7; 146:5).

- What other truths about God's promises and character can you cling to right now?

- How did others in the Bible who struggled with disappointment find hope in God as their foundational strength (see 2 Cor. 4:8)?

- Can you think of past situations in your own life when you trusted God through disappointment? What was that process like, and what did you learn?

- What does the Bible say about how God uses disappointment as the path to future blessing for ourselves and for others (see 2 Cor. 1:3–7)?

- What deeper truths may God be trying to reveal to help you grow?

- What loving conviction might God be offering?
- What emotions do you feel after seeing God's truth about the situation?

Create a brief statement about what you discovered in *discern* (see page 119 for an example).

Decide

- How have your own decisions contributed to the disappointment, and as a result, what needs to be confessed to God and others?
- Which part of this situation is out of your control? How can you release this to God?
- If there are other people involved in this situation, is God calling you to speak to them about what you're feeling or is He encouraging you to process and release the hurt just to Him?
- What self-care rituals can you practice right now to help yourself work through the disappointment?
- What other actions can you take to be released from the pain of the disappointment?
- Do you sense the presence of *pachad* fear or *yirah* fear (see chap. 8)? If so, how might God want you to handle this fear?
- What other spiritually centered activities, like prayer and worship, can you practice to surround yourself with God's loving presence in order to be released from the disappointment?
- How may God be calling you to *not* take any action steps but trust in His ability to work all things out for your good?
- How is God calling you to acknowledge the disappointment but also stand firmly in expectant hope?
- Where will you decide to emotionally dwell? Of what biblical truths will you remind yourself?

Create a brief statement about what you discovered in *decide* (see page 138 for an example).

ADD Statement

Combine each of the statements from the ADD sections into a single affirmation. Here's an example in both condensed and expanded form:

Condensed Version

Acknowledge: "I am extremely disappointed in my relationships with my adult kids. This disappointment is understandable because I've always wanted to have close connections with them, and it seems like they're so different from me."

Discern: "Yes, it's true that my kids have distanced themselves and even done things that have left me disillusioned about our ability to be close as an extended family; however, it's not true that they don't love me or that they don't want me involved in their lives."

Decide: "Therefore, in light of these truths, I will remind myself that I am not responsible for their actions. I am responsible for two things: my actions toward them and my perspective on the situation. God loves me and wants to use me as an instrument of healing, so I will be obedient to love my kids right now where they're at, and I will be thankful for the relationship we do have."

Expanded Version

Acknowledge: "I've been feeling sad lately, and I realize that I am extremely disappointed in my relationships with my adult kids. This disappointment is understandable because I've always wanted to have close connections with my kids, and it seems like they're so different from me. It makes me wonder if I'm a good enough parent or if I did something wrong in raising them. I'm fearful that we will lose touch or that I won't be able to participate in my grandchildren's lives. I'm thankful that, because of Jesus's own experiences of being hurt by friends, as in the case of Judas and Peter, He understands how much it hurts to see relationships turn out differently than we expect."

Discern: "Yes, it's true that my kids have distanced themselves and even done things that have left me disillusioned about our ability to be close as an extended family; however, it's not true that they don't love me or that they don't want me involved in their lives. It's also not true that I pushed them away or that I was a bad parent. The Bible reminds me of many stories of children who turned out very different than their parents expected, such as the biblical story of the prodigal son. I'm also reminded that God has made us all unique and that we can love each other despite our differences. It gives me comfort that I can play a part in growing our family bonds by letting God's love flow through me."

Decide: "Therefore, I'll remind myself that I am not responsible for their actions. I am responsible for two things: my actions toward them and my perspective on the situation. I will also remember that God doesn't make mistakes in how He brings people together. He uses us to encourage and 'sharpen' one another (Prov. 27:17). Therefore, I will continue to release my disappointment to Him as I see it surfacing, and I will trust in the work He's doing in our family. I will choose to wait with great expectation, focusing on the good things ahead. I will remember that God loves me and wants to use me as an instrument of healing, so I will be obedient to love my kids where they're at right now, and I will be thankful for the relationship we do have."

11

Worry

Worry feels so hard to manage because it taps into one of our strongest human desires—our need for control. I once heard worry described as "going into the future without God," and I believe that sums it up perfectly. We want to know the future right now so that we can rest assured that all will be well. Since only God knows the future, worry is our human attempt to be in charge of our own destiny. Worry is understandable and reasonable in the face of frightening events, which is why we can admit to feeling worried but still lean into trust. That doesn't mean that the worry disappears immediately, but what if worry is our invitation to trust God?

Many of us chastise ourselves for dealing with worry. We think, *Why can't I just let this go and trust God?* When we recognize worry as a reasonable amygdala response designed to keep us safe, we can manage it in a healthier way. The more often we use worry when facing stress, the more often our brain—which thrives on patterns and repetition—will default to it.

Instead of trying to escape the worry, we can acknowledge why it is present and ask ourselves how our mind is trying to use worry to keep us safe. We can turn down the dial on worry instead of trying to eliminate it. Journaling can be extremely helpful for processing worry because writing the words down moves the worrisome thoughts from the deepest parts of our mind onto paper, allowing our logical mind to see and analyze what we're thinking.

Kindness and curiosity are incredibly important, too, since worry needs to be lovingly acknowledged before it can be released. We can soothe our worry instead of scorning it. Thankfully our loving Savior models how to do this as He comforts our trembling hearts. The deeper we grow in understanding His perfect love, the easier it is to let go of fear and worry (1 John 4:18).

It's true that God tells us *not* to worry, but He also understands *why* we worry. Jesus Himself promised that we'd have trouble in this world and acknowledged worry as a natural response (John 16:33). He encourages us to renew our fearful thoughts by surrendering them to God and refocusing our mind on gratitude (Phil. 4:4–6). When we find ourselves drowning in deep waters of fear and concern, He reaches His hand out to pull us from the chaos and to set us in a safe place (Ps. 18:16–19). He asks us to trust Him and release the worry, even when things don't make sense.

It's also important to note that, for some, worry can be rooted in other mental health conditions, such as an anxiety disorder. If you feel like anxiety is a consistent part of your emotional struggle, seek the help of a mental health professional for insight.

When worry comes calling, we get to decide if we will accept His invitation to release the what-if questions, or if we will stay stuck in the mire, trying to micromanage the situation and figure it out on our own. He may not immediately calm the storm around us, but if we choose to release worry to God, He has the power to calm the storm within us.

Questions for Discovery

Acknowledge

- What specific thoughts of worry are you experiencing?
- To whom (or about what situation) is the worry directed?

- How might the worry relate to not having your core needs met, such as a need for provision or acceptance?
- Is your worry a surface-level emotion or a secondary emotion? If it's a secondary emotion, what other emotions may be present?
- After examining the evidence, why does it make sense that you're worried? Consider the compassionate words you'd share with a loved one who was feeling this type of worry, then speak them over your situation.
- Although God does not want us to worry, how might He comfort you with His understanding about why you are worried? Consider specific Bible verses, Bible stories, and examples from your past that comfort you with signs of His provision.

Create a brief statement about what you discovered in *acknowledge* (see page 103 for an example).

Discern

- How might a lack of self-care be heightening the intensity of your worry? Ask yourself the following questions:
  - ▶ Have I eaten something nutritious lately?
  - ▶ Have I had enough water today?
  - ▶ Have I moved my body recently?
  - ▶ Have I been getting enough sleep?
  - ▶ Do I have other complex or frustrating emotions inside me that need to be processed?
  - ▶ How might environmental or hormonal changes be contributing to the intensity?
- What filters may you be using to process your worry? For example:
  - ▶ Are you using black-and-white thinking to process the worry?
  - ▶ Is your worry causing you to believe lies or half-truths about the situation?

- ▸ Is your worry rooted in the assumption that someone will act in an unhelpful way or in a belief that the situation will never change?

- ▸ How might the fighter, runner, freezer, or pleaser personas be present as you're processing?

- ▸ How might worry's threat to core needs impact how you're processing the truth of this situation?

- ▸ Based on what you discovered, why does it make sense that you may be using these filters to process the worry?

- If the worry is about a person or a situation, what aspects of this circumstance can you control?

- What does God say about how to handle worry (see Ps. 37:1; Prov. 12:25; Matt. 6:25–34; Luke 12:25–27)?

- What does the Bible say about putting your hope in God as a way to manage worry (see Ps. 130:5–6; Phil. 4:6; 1 Pet. 3:14)?

- What deeper truths may God be trying to reveal to help you grow?

- What loving conviction might God be offering?

- What emotions do you feel after seeing God's truth about the situation?

Create a brief statement about what you discovered in *discern* **(see page 119 for an example).**

Decide

- How have your own decisions contributed to the worry, and as a result, what needs to be confessed to God or others?

- Which part of this situation is out of your control? How can you release this to God?

- If there are other people involved in this situation, is God calling you to speak to them about what you're feeling or is He encouraging you to process and release the hurt just to Him?

- What self-care rituals can you practice right now to help yourself work through the worry?
- Do you sense the presence of *pachad* fear or *yirah* fear (see chap. 8)? If so, how might God want you to handle this fear?
- What other spiritually centered activities, like prayer and worship, can you do to surround yourself with God's loving presence in order to be released from the worry?
- How may God be calling you to rest in His ability to work all things out for your good in this situation?
- Where will you decide to emotionally dwell? Of what biblical truths will you remind yourself?

Create a brief statement about what you discovered in *decide* (see page 138 for an example).

ADD Statement

Combine each of the statements from the ADD sections into a single affirmation. Here's an example in both condensed and expanded form:

Condensed Version

Acknowledge: "It makes sense that I'm worried about my job, but my attempt to work harder to prove myself is not helping. My worry is understandable, but it's stealing my peace and hurting my family."

Discern: "It's true that God is asking me to release worry and to trust Him in this situation. It's not true that I can control this situation by micromanaging all the details and worrying about provision. It is true that He is faithful and He's asking me to stop trying to control things and to rest in His loving sovereignty."

Decide: "I will work hard, but I release the outcome of this to God. When I feel worry creeping in, I will remind myself that I can surrender my worries to Him. I will not let anything, including my own fears, steal the peace that God wants to provide when I focus my thoughts on Him (Isa. 26:3)."

Expanded Version

Acknowledge: "Lately I've been really worried about losing my job. This makes sense because several people have been laid off, and I see our company's sales dropping. I've been trying to take charge of the situation by working longer hours and trying to prove my value to the team, but all it's doing is feeding my need to control the situation. It's understandable that the worry is there because I am afraid I will no longer be able to provide; however, this worry causes me to be burned-out and exhausted when I get home, and my personal life is suffering."

Discern: "God wants me to surrender this situation to Him, not try to control it by working harder. The truth is that I am not in charge of whether or not I lose my job. Worry is only making me more stressed and is causing damage to my personal life and relationships. It's not true that God will abandon me and not take care of my needs. He has proven Himself faithful in the past. Isaiah 30:18 reminds me that He blesses those who wait for His help, so even when things look bleak, I will look to Him as my help instead of my own efforts."

Decide: "Therefore, I am going to give my best at work, but I am releasing the need to work frenetically in an attempt to prove myself. Today I have a job, and that is what I will focus on. I will apologize to my family and friends for giving them my emotional leftovers lately. I will look around for other job openings in case things go sideways, but I will relinquish my worry about provision to my capable Savior. When worry threatens to steal my peace, I will remind myself of how my God has always, always faithfully provided, and I will refocus my thoughts back on His promises to keep me in perfect peace when I focus on His truth. In fact, I am going to start a journal to track His faithfulness to our family over the years. He is in charge, and I will not allow my own worry about what 'could be' steal the gift of peace that God wants to give me right now."

12

Shame

We've all felt that horrible pang in our stomachs known as shame. When we've committed sin, shame and guilt can be signs of God's loving conviction. Conviction is healthy because it helps us see where we are not following God so that we can repent from our behavior and change our ways (Ps. 119:39). The Bible encourages us to confess any sin and to let the Spirit renew our minds so that we can live in the holiness Christ achieved on our behalf (Eph. 4:21–24). Although God doesn't want to rub our noses in our mistakes, He allows us to feel the heaviness of shame through conviction so that we will confess anything that could get in the way of our relationship with Him and others (Ps. 32:3–4; 2 Cor. 7:10).

Shame can also be the result of condemnation, which is one of the enemy's tactics to keep us from walking in the daily gift of victory in Christ. Condemnation is present when we hear any negative inner voices that say we're bad, that we can't do anything right, or that we're without any hope for change. This scathing, accusatory voice doesn't offer a way out but only wants to drag us down into despair. Condemnation keeps us focused on the weight of our sin and shame without any chance of forgiveness or restoration.

The enemy's assaultive and harsh voice of condemnation is a sharp contrast to God's assertive but helpful voice of conviction. From its language to its tone, condemnation is designed to steal, kill, and destroy, while conviction is designed to lead us back to full and abundant living.

Thankfully, as children of God, we don't have to listen to the voice of condemnation. Once we choose to stop running from sin and we confess it to God, we can know that we are forgiven, and our guilt is gone! Christ's sacrifice guarantees that we are without condemnation from God (Rom. 8:1). In addition, confession takes away the power of the enemy's ammo as he tries to accuse us. We can say, "Yes, I did that, but I confessed it and God has forgiven me. Move on, Satan!"

If we have chosen to accept Christ's sacrifice as the covering for our sins and we've dedicated our lives to following His leading and example, then we can boldly release shame because we know that God is not angry at us (1 Thess. 5:9). Like any relationship, we do need to be quick to repent and ask God for forgiveness when we make a mistake in order to keep our fellowship strong. But once we do that, we can know He has lifted the burden of shame, and we can move forward in freedom.

But what if we still *feel* guilty and ashamed despite logically knowing that we are forgiven? We can lean into the *discern* step where we discover the truth about our forgiveness, and in *decide*, we can choose to emotionally dwell in His promised forgiveness over our guilty feelings (1 John 3:10).

Will we apologize, repent, and accept God's offer of forgiveness? Or will we allow ourselves to wallow in the icky feeling of shame, convincing ourselves that we are in fact horrible, helpless, and without hope? We get to decide. Like with the woman caught in adultery in John 8:1–11, Christ did not come to condemn us but to set us free, and that includes freedom from any voice that stands to accuse us. We choose which voice we will listen to.

Questions for Discovery

Acknowledge

- What specific thoughts of shame are you experiencing?
- To whom (or about what situation) is the shame directed?
- How might the shame relate to not having your core needs met, such as a need for belonging or control?
- Is your shame a surface-level emotion or a secondary emotion? If it's a secondary emotion, what other emotions may be present?
- After examining the evidence, why does it make sense that you're feeling shame? Consider the compassionate words you'd share with a loved one who was feeling this type of shame, then speak them over your situation.
- Although God will not justify sin committed in shame, how might He comfort you with His understanding about why you are lonely? Consider specific Bible verses, Bible stories, and examples from your past that show His care for you.

Create a brief statement about what you discovered in *acknowledge* (see page 103 for an example).

Discern

- Is what you're feeling healthy conviction from God or harmful condemnation from the enemy? What can you cite as evidence?
- How might a lack of self-care be making it harder to process these feelings of shame, like condemnation or conviction? Ask yourself the following questions:
  - Have I eaten something nutritious lately?
  - Have I had enough water today?
  - Have I moved my body recently?
  - Have I been getting enough sleep?

- ▸ Do I have other complex or frustrating emotions inside me that need to be processed?
- ▸ How might environmental or hormonal changes be contributing to the intensity?
- Are there other past actions, such as other sins you've committed or other painful experiences that may or may not have been caused by you, that are triggered by this shame? How do these add to the emotions you're feeling?
- If there are any secondary emotions present, such as disappointment or anger, what biblical truth can you remind yourself of in order to release yourself from these other emotions?
- If you're feeling conviction, how would God want you to respond (see Lev. 5:5; 2 Chron. 7:14; Ps. 32:1–7; James 5:16)?
- If you're feeling condemnation, how would God want you to respond (see Ps. 34:5; Rom. 8:1; 2 Cor. 3:17; 1 John 3:10)?
- What deeper truths may God be trying to reveal to help you grow?
- What loving conviction might God be offering?
- What emotions do you feel after seeing God's truth about the situation?

Create a brief statement about what you discovered in *discern* (see page 119 for an example).

Decide

- How have your own decisions contributed to the feelings of shame, and as a result, what needs to be confessed to God or others?
- Which part of this situation is out of your control? How can you release this to God?
- If there are other people involved in this situation, is God calling you to speak to them about what you're feeling or

is He encouraging you to process and release the hurt just to Him?

- What self-care rituals can you practice right now to help yourself work through the shame?
- Do you sense the presence of *pachad* fear or *yirah* fear (see chap. 8)? If so, how might God want you to handle this fear?
- What other spiritually centered activities, like prayer and worship, can you do to surround yourself with God's loving presence in order to be released from shame?
- How may God be calling you to rest in His ability to work all things out for your good in this situation?
- Where will you decide to emotionally dwell? Of what biblical truths will you remind yourself?

Create a brief statement about what you discovered in *decide* (see page 138 for an example).

ADD Statement

Combine each of the statements from the ADD sections into a single affirmation. Here's an example in both condensed and expanded form:

Condensed Version

Acknowledge: "It makes sense why shame creeps in because I did make some bad choices in my past. I often feel 'less than,' and I don't know how to shake these feelings, even though I know that I've been forgiven in Christ."

Discern: "It's true that I struggled with alcohol addiction and that I hurt others in that process. It's also true that I am forgiven in Christ and my entire life has changed. I'm no longer a slave to my past but fully redeemed because of Christ's sacrifice for me."

Decide: "Therefore when I hear condemning thoughts about my worth or my past sins, I will focus on the reality that my faith in Christ has washed me clean. God has given me a beautiful new path forward, and I will fix my thoughts on His promises for me."

Expanded Version

Acknowledge: "I can't seem to shake the feeling that because of my past I am not good enough. As an addict, I made some really bad choices in my former life, and I hurt many people. Now I'm following Christ and I've asked God to forgive me of my past mistakes, but I still struggle with feeling 'less than,' and I'm tired of it. I want to walk in freedom and not feel condemned anymore."

Discern: "Yes, it's true that I allowed alcohol to run my life for years. It's true that I ignored God's opportunities to change and that I hurt my brother, my parents, and even my little girl with my destructive behavior. But it's also true that now I live differently. Like David says in Psalm 40, my life has been lifted from the muck and mire, and God has set my feet upon a new rock and made my footsteps firm. I am clean and fully restored! It's true that none of us are perfect. Romans 3:23 says that we've all fallen short of God's glory, and that we're not expected to save ourselves. Hallelujah that Christ paid the ransom to rescue me from my mistakes. I am free in Him!"

Decide: "Therefore, when I hear that inner voice say that I am not worthy, that I am broken, or that I am flawed, I will stand on the promise that I answer only to God, and that I am forgiven because of my faith in Christ. I am in charge of what thoughts I reinforce in my mind, and I will not allow myself to play with any toxic thoughts that try to hold me back from the righteous, redeemed, abundant life that Christ has given me. I will stay committed to Him through daily prayer and Bible reading and through listening to how I can best follow His guidelines for living. When I feel especially weak in this area, I will ask God for the strength and clarity to release condemnation and stand in the fullness of my new identity."

13

Discontentment

Discontentment—a socially polite word for what the Bible calls *coveting*—can catch any of us off guard. We can be having a perfectly good day when *boom!* We find ourselves emotionally unsettled after scrolling through someone else's perfectly curated family photos.

Why are we so easily ensnared by discontentment's trap? One reason is that we experience our flawed lives in high definition while viewing others' circumstances through a sanitized, color-corrected lens. Life regularly reminds us of our own blatant faults—and those of our loved ones—along with what can feel like a never-ending affront of frustrating, unfair circumstances that we can't always understand or change. While comparison itself isn't a terrible thing, especially if we're positively inspired by others' actions, it can quickly breed discontentment when it leads us away from happily accepting our current reality.

Discontentment plays off our need for justice. It capitalizes on a deep insecurity that we won't get all our needs met and that we really aren't as loved by God as someone else. When we're lost in discontentment, we're not enjoying the gift of the moment but instead drowning in an it's-not-fair pity party. If we continue to believe we've been denied our rightful due, we allow our discontentment to grow into jealousy, anger, and resentment that not only influences our take on the world but can even drive us to hurt others.

Discontentment can convince us that even the most morally reprehensible actions are justifiable. Cain murdered his brother Abel because he was jealous of God's approval of Abel's gift (Gen. 4:2–12). Sarah treated Hagar harshly and drove her away because she was jealous of Hagar's ability to bear children for Abraham (Gen. 16:1–6). Joseph's brothers sold him into slavery because they were jealous that Joseph was more loved by their father (Gen. 37:2–28).

Discern is a powerful step in working through discontentment. When we are able to get out of our I've-been-slighted emotional brain and into the clarity of our logical mind, we can better manage discontentment's full-frontal attack. As we work through *discern*, we can remind ourselves first that we will never have the full picture of a person's sorrows and happiness unless we can somehow walk in their shoes (Prov. 14:10). No person is perfectly happy with every part of their lives—we all know *that* woman with the perfect body who's still discontent with her looks—so we can stop pretending that "they" have it "better" than us, even if it looks like they're going through an easier time. In addition, we can remember that God knows every detail of our lives, promises to take care of all our needs—though not necessarily all our wants—and gives us the perfect allotment necessary for our situation.[1] I've found this truth easier to accept the longer I have walked with Christ and seen His faithful, consistent provision for every single need in all my life seasons.

God is good and He is faithful. These truths are easy to believe when we're flush with money, enjoying perfect health, and walking on a tropical beach hand in hand with the love of our life. Discontentment promises us that we need that idyllic life to be happy, but God's Word promises that we can be content whatever the circumstances and that *we* are in charge of managing our own

182

contentment levels by keeping our thoughts fixed on His truth (Isa. 26:3; Phil. 4:8–11; 1 Tim. 6:6).

That's why ongoing, habitual gratitude is also a wonderful anecdote when discontentment comes knocking. When we regularly recognize the fingerprints of a good God in our lives—not just as a theoretical concept but as a reality—our perspective changes. We can acknowledge that we're feeling discontent—or gasp, even covetous!—and remind that unsettled inner voice that we have everything we need as a well-cared-for child of the King. Discontentment can even be a reminder to turn to Christ for our fulfillment since only He can provide the eternal satisfaction we seek.

Questions for Discovery

Acknowledge

- What specific thoughts of discontentment (or jealousy) are you experiencing?
- To whom (or about what situation) are the discontented thoughts directed?
- What other related emotions might be hiding underneath your feelings of discontentment?
- How might the discontentment relate to not having your core needs met, such as a need for belonging or success?
- Is your discontentment a surface-level emotion or a secondary emotion? If it's a secondary emotion, what other emotions may be present?
- After examining the evidence, why does it make sense that you're discontented? Consider the compassionate words you'd share with a loved one who was feeling this type of discontentment, then speak them over your situation.
- Although God will not justify sin committed in discontentment, how might He comfort you with His understanding about why you are discontented? Consider

specific Bible verses, Bible stories, and examples from your past that show His care for you.

Create a brief statement about what you discovered in *acknowledge* **(see page 103 for an example).**

Discern

- How might a lack of self-care be heightening the intensity of your discontentment? Ask yourself the following questions:
  - ▸ Have I eaten something nutritious lately?
  - ▸ Have I had enough water today?
  - ▸ Have I moved my body recently?
  - ▸ Have I been getting enough sleep?
  - ▸ Do I have other complex or frustrating emotions inside me that need to be processed?
  - ▸ How might environmental or hormonal changes be contributing to the intensity?
- What filters may you be using to process your discontentment? For example:
  - ▸ Are you using black-and-white thinking to process the discontentment?
  - ▸ Is your discontentment causing you to believe lies or half-truths about the situation?
  - ▸ Is your discontentment rooted in the lie that your circumstances will never change?
  - ▸ How might the fighter, runner, freezer, or pleaser personas be present as you're processing?
  - ▸ How might discontentment's threat to core needs impact how you're processing the truth of this situation?
  - ▸ Based on what you discovered, why does it make sense that you may be using these filters to process the discontentment?

- How does understanding the reality that no situation or person's life is perfect help you release your discontentment?
- What does the Bible say about how jealousy affects a person (see Prov. 14:30; 27:4)?
- What does Scripture say about the potential consequences of unmanaged discontentment (see Gen. 4:2–8; 30:1–24; Job 5:2; Prov. 6:32–35; 1 Cor. 3:3; James 3:15–16; 4:2)?
- How does God want us to handle discontentment or jealousy (see Gal. 5:24–26; Phil. 4:11; James 4:2; 1 Pet. 2:1; 1 Tim. 6:6–8)?
- How have you seen God provide for your needs in the past, perhaps in similar ways? What did you learn about His provision from those situations?
- What deeper truths may God be trying to reveal to help you grow?
- What loving conviction might God be offering?
- What emotions do you feel after seeing God's truth about the situation?

Create a brief statement about what you discovered in *discern* (see page 119 for an example).

Decide

- How have your own decisions contributed to the discontentment, and as a result, what needs to be confessed to God or others?
- Which part of this situation is out of your control? How can you release this to God?
- If there are other people involved in this situation, is God calling you to speak to them about what you're feeling or is He encouraging you to process and release the hurt just to Him?

- What self-care rituals can you practice right now to help yourself work through the discontentment?
- Do you sense the presence of *pachad* fear or *yirah* fear (see chap. 8)? If so, how might God want you to handle this fear?
- What other spiritually centered activities, like prayer and worship, can you practice to surround yourself with God's loving presence in order to be released from the discontentment?
- How may God be calling you to rest in His ability to work all things out for your good in this situation?
- Where will you decide to emotionally dwell? Of what biblical truths will you remind yourself?

Create a brief statement about what you discovered in *decide* (see page 138 for an example).

ADD Statement

Combine each of the statements from the ADD sections into a single affirmation. Here's an example in both condensed and expanded form:

Condensed Version

Acknowledge: "It makes sense that I feel discontentment in my marriage right now and that I'm jealous of my friends' marriages, because my spouse has been withdrawn lately and this hurts me."

Discern: "While it's true that lately he has chosen to spend more time gaming than with me, I won't believe the lie that he doesn't love me. He's not pulling away from me, but he's processing the difficult news about his brother by going off into his own world for a while."

Decide: "I'm going to let my husband know how I'm feeling. I'm also going to see if we can plan a time away to reconnect. It's important that I allow God to fill my needs for companionship and love during this time as well, so I'm going to make extra time for prayer, journaling, and meditating on His promises."

Expanded Version

Acknowledge: "It feels like everyone else has a perfect marriage with no problems while I'm unhappy with how my husband treats me. This makes me jealous of other married people I know, especially when I hear about their wonderful weekends away with their spouses. When my husband is home from work, he seems more into gaming than into spending time with me, and this really hurts because I haven't seen him much lately and spending time together is my love language. The romance is gone, and I'm left feeling unfulfilled. We could have so much more if he would just change!"

Discern: "It's true that our relationship isn't as close as it could be and that I have good reason to be discontented. It's true that we don't spend as much time together as we used to; however, it's also true that he's a good man and that he loves me. I see that he's been really withdrawn since his brother has been sick, and he's managing his feelings by escaping into his gaming time. I hate that this is our reality because I feel like I'm being cheated of his affection, but I also see that his pulling away has nothing to do with me. He is in survival mode, and he's not intending to hurt me."

Decide: "In light of these truths, I will find a time this weekend (before he starts playing his games) to speak to my husband about what I'm feeling. I need to be reassured of his love for me. I need to be reminded that his pulling away is not about anything I've done. And I'll let him know that it makes sense that he's concerned about his brother's terminal illness, and I'll remind him that I'm here to support him through this. I'll also ask if we can plan an upcoming time to get away for the weekend to reconnect. Since I recognize that he can't meet all my needs for love and affection even in the most ideal conditions, I'll make sure that I'm spending extra time with God and reflecting regularly on His love for me that never runs out."

14

Loneliness

God says it's not good for us to be alone. Even from the beginning of creation, God recognized our human need to be in community and to be understood by others (Gen. 2:18). While we all have different needs for alone time, Ecclesiastes 4:9–11 speaks of the practical virtues of *not* being alone, and the apostle Paul regularly wrote about fellowship as a gift among believers that keeps the church healthy (Acts 2:42; Rom. 15:24; Heb. 10:25). In the Bible, loneliness is associated with times of deep distress and pain, but verses like Proverbs 25:24 also cheekily remind us that loneliness is better than being around someone who's difficult to live with.

Loneliness can be especially excruciating when it's thrust upon us uninvited. The COVID-19 pandemic had severe effects on our society's mental health as a whole, especially among teens.[1] Loneliness surged during this period and continues to be a health crisis, according to the US Surgeon General.[2] It makes sense: when we're isolated and alone, not only are we away from the blessings of social connection but we no longer have the buffers of busyness to distract us from our pain.

While loneliness can be extremely painful, being alone can also be an opportunity for focused concentration and spiritual growth. During the COVID-19 pandemic, many came face-to-face with their need for God, and after the lockdown ended several revivals sprang up on college campuses.[3] The Bible records many instances of miracles and supernatural events occurring during times of solitude: Moses was wandering alone when God spoke to him from the burning bush (Exod. 3:1–6); Daniel was alone when he received a powerful vision of the preincarnate Christ (Dan. 10:4–19); and John the Baptist spent time alone in the wilderness (Luke 1:80). Jesus was led by the Spirit into the desert to be alone for forty days before He began His public ministry, and He often went off to be alone before God.

Even in the moments when we feel left out and uninvited, God is always with us (Ps. 139). We cannot escape His presence (John 14:18). We don't carry our burdens alone, as God promises to be our partner when we feel overwhelmed by life's difficulties (Matt. 11:28). He not only sets prisoners free and restores their lives but places those who are lonely in community with others (Ps. 68:6). Next to our salvation, God's comfort for our lonely, weary hearts is one of the greatest gifts of being a Christian.

Questions for Discovery

Acknowledge

- What specific thoughts of loneliness are you experiencing?
- To whom (or about what situation) is the loneliness directed?
- What events, people, or other life circumstances are causing this surge in loneliness?
- How might the loneliness relate to not having your core needs met, such as a need for belonging?
- Is your loneliness a surface-level emotion or a secondary emotion? If it's a secondary emotion, what other emotions may be present?

- After examining the evidence, why does it make sense that you're lonely? Consider the compassionate words you'd share with a loved one who was feeling this type of loneliness, then speak them over your situation.

- Although God will not justify sin committed in loneliness, how might He comfort you with His understanding about why you are lonely? Consider specific Bible verses, Bible stories, and examples from your past that show His care for you.

Create a brief statement about what you discovered in *acknowledge* (see page 103 for an example).

Discern

- How might a lack of self-care be heightening the intensity of your loneliness? Ask yourself the following questions:
  - ▸ Have I eaten something nutritious lately?
  - ▸ Have I had enough water today?
  - ▸ Have I moved my body recently?
  - ▸ Have I been getting enough sleep?
  - ▸ Do I have other complex or frustrating emotions inside me that need to be processed?
  - ▸ How might environmental or hormonal changes be contributing to the intensity?[4]

- What filters may you be using to process your loneliness? For example:
  - ▸ Are you using black-and-white thinking to process the loneliness?
  - ▸ Is your loneliness causing you to believe lies or half-truths about the situation?
  - ▸ How might the fighter, runner, freezer, or pleaser personas be present as you're processing?
  - ▸ How might loneliness's threat to core needs impact how you're processing the truth of this situation?

- ‣ Based on what you discovered, why does it make sense that you may be using these filters to process the loneliness?
- Read Psalm 139:1–16, 2 Corinthians 4:8–9, and John 14:18 to hear about God's promise to be with His people at all times. How do these verses comfort you in your loneliness?
- How does God promise to help us in our loneliness (see Gen. 2:18; Ps. 68:6; John 6:37; Rev. 3:20)?
- How has God offered you comfort in the past when you felt alone? How may God be using this time to grow your fellowship with Him?
- While it is not always comfortable to be lonely, what deeper truths may God be trying to reveal during this period? How does this perspective help you process your loneliness?
- What loving conviction might God be offering?
- What emotions do you feel after seeing God's truth about the situation?

Create a brief statement about what you discovered in *discern* (see page 119 for an example).

Decide

- How have your own decisions contributed to the loneliness, and as a result, what needs to be confessed to God or others?
- Which part of this situation is out of your control? How can you release this to God?
- If there are other people involved in this situation, is God calling you to speak to them about what you're feeling or is He encouraging you to process and release the hurt just to Him?
- What self-care rituals can you practice right now to help yourself work through the loneliness?

- Do you sense the presence of *pachad* fear or *yirah* fear (see chap. 8)? If so, how might God want you to handle this fear?

- What other spiritually centered activities, like prayer and worship, can you practice to surround yourself with God's loving presence to be released from the loneliness?

- How may God be calling you to rest in His ability to work all things out for your good in this situation?

- Where will you decide to emotionally dwell? Of what biblical truths will you remind yourself?

Create a brief statement about what you discovered in *decide* (see page 138 for an example).

ADD Statement

Combine each of the statements from the ADD sections into a single affirmation. Here's an example in both condensed and expanded form:

Condensed Version

Acknowledge: "I hate feeling so lonely around the other parents from my son's basketball team. It makes sense that I'm closed off from them because I have had bad experiences in the past with other team parents, and these people seem very cliquish. I am leery of opening myself up and getting hurt again, and this is a natural defense mechanism."

Discern: "It's true that I have been hurt, but it's also true that these basketball parents aren't the ones who hurt me. I am isolating myself and only increasing my loneliness by not taking a risk and opening up."

Decide: "I am in charge here. If I remain aloof with these people, then I can't expect them to be friendly with me, especially since many of them have been close for years. I'd like to make these practices and games as pleasant as possible, so I will open up and start conversations with them and see where it goes. Even if these men and women are rude to me, my confidence is in God, and I am not defined by whether or not I'm a part of their social club."

Expanded Version

Acknowledge: "Going to my son's basketball practices and games has become torturous for me lately, and it's because I feel like I don't fit in with the other parents. They plan many get-togethers and never invite me. It makes me feel like I'm in junior high again being rejected by the popular kids—ugh! These parents are the reasons I have zero self-esteem at the games and don't say a word to any of them. My heart can't take the rejection again, so I just grit my teeth and ignore their chitter-chatter around me."

Discern: "It's true that I've been hurt by others and that I'm still nursing those wounds, but it's not fair to assume that these parents don't like me. They did not cause the damage that makes me feel insecure around new people. It's normal for people who know each other to talk more at the games, and that's what they're doing. My choice to stay silent and not speak to them isn't helping the situation either. Maybe they think that I'm not very friendly and they are keeping their distance. They do seem cliquish, but my quietness could be viewed as rudeness too. Also, I know that my identity is not found in what others think of me but in who I am in Christ."

Decide: "In light of these truths, I get to choose how to interpret and respond to this situation. First, I don't have to identify their actions as a personal insult. If I remain aloof with them, I can't expect them to be friendly in return, especially since many of them have known each other for a while. I will rely on God to help me take a risk and step out of my shell even though it's uncomfortable. I am tired of feeling like this every time we go to practices or games, so I'm going to make an effort to start conversations and see where it goes. Even if they decide to be rude, I will stand strong in my confidence as God's child. That is what defines my identity, and it cannot be taken from me."

15

What about Overwhelm and Exhaustion?

Isn't it interesting how frequently we describe ourselves as being overwhelmed or exhausted? These emotions are often used as cultural catchall phrases to describe when we're swamped with unpleasant emotions and don't know where to start!

While overwhelm is very real and deserves to be analyzed, it often shows up as a surface-level emotion that needs calming, soothing, and deciphering in order to process the root-level emotion behind it. We can walk through a mini version of ADD in order to process that emotional iceberg and discover what's underneath.

First, if we're stuck in heightened emotions, we can use an emotional prep tool to bring peace to the situation and calm our spirits so we can use ADD more effectively.

Once peace is established, then we can assess why we're struggling with these feelings by asking questions like:

- Why does it make sense that I'm struggling with overwhelm or exhaustion based on my current circumstances?
- What painful or difficult emotions are resulting from my current situations? How can I offer myself compassion for feeling those?

196

Next, we can discern what type of overwhelm or exhaustion we're experiencing by examining each part of our self (emotional, intellectual, physical, and spiritual). We can ask:

- Am I physically exhausted and in need of sleep or rest?
- Am I mentally exhausted and looking for relief from the inner noise?
- Am I socially exhausted and in need of recharging my social batteries?
- Am I on sensory overload, meaning that I feel overly stimulated, and in need of quiet?
- Am I spiritually drained and needing God to revive my hope and sense of purpose?

It may be tempting to answer yes to all the above questions, and they may, in fact, all be true. It's more productive, however, when we determine which part of self is in greatest need of tender loving care and start there. We can always go back and repeat this process later to bring help to other parts of our self that feel overwhelmed or weary.

Since this book explores emotional confidence, let's talk about some practical tools for emotional overwhelm and exhaustion. We can discern our next best step by asking ourselves, *What do I need to be emotionally filled up?* Consider each of these solutions:

If you need silence and solace . . . Do whatever you can to get into a quiet place at your earliest convenience. It doesn't have to be a perfect, Zen environment with minimalistic decorating and potted succulents. It just needs to be a place where you can find stillness and little noise. If messy, unorganized spaces make it hard for you to calm down, choose an area with little visual distraction, even if that's only one corner of your home. Being in nature is great too. Or going for a drive by yourself with the music off. Silence the cacophony of inner voices by allowing yourself to sit and wait in the quiet, perhaps utilizing some emotional prep tools like box breathing.

If you need reassurance and comfort . . . It's normal to feel especially raw and vulnerable when struggling with emotional overwhelm. Maybe you can't begin to process all that you're feeling yet,

Bible Verses to Help with Overwhelm and Exhaustion

2 Samuel 22:30	Psalm 84:5
2 Samuel 22:40	Proverbs 3:5–8
Psalm 18:32	Isaiah 30:15
Psalm 23:3	Isaiah 40:29
Psalm 28:7–8	1 Corinthians 1:25
Psalm 46:1	2 Corinthians 1:8–11
Psalm 73:26	

and you simply need God's loving presence. As a kind and good Father, He is more than happy to calm your fears and comfort you with His promises. A friend of mine has a sign that reads "Everything will be all right. Maybe not today but eventually," and that's the place God holds us when we're overwhelmed. Prayer, Bible reading, meditation, and journaling are extremely helpful here.

If you need to expend energy . . . When you feel almost jittery with anxiety-inducing, overwhelming emotions, consider how to use your body to physically move that electric energy out of your system. Depending on your preferences and your body's abilities, that could look like doing yoga, walking, running, lifting weights, or just turning on upbeat music and dancing in the kitchen.

Once you feel centered and have worked through the overwhelm and exhaustion a bit, it's time to consider what other emotions are underneath and use ADD to work through what you discover.

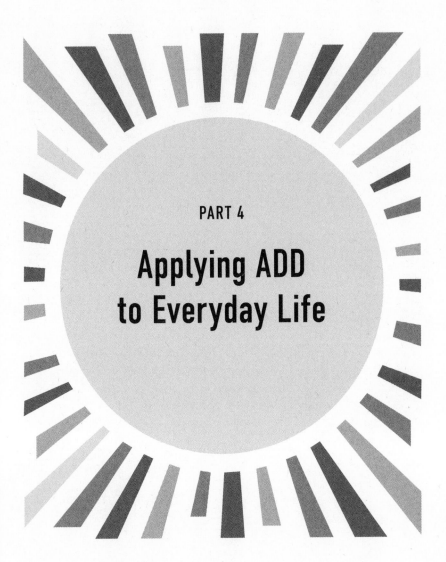

PART 4

Applying ADD to Everyday Life

16

Using ADD to Better Manage Emotions in Relationships

Some of the most taxing and painful emotions we will experience are those associated with our closest relationships. Whether between a husband and wife, siblings, or a parent and child, negative emotions that stem from relationship hurts are some of the hardest feelings to manage, especially when the afflictions build and are not resolved. We look to relationships as our emotional anchors in an uncertain world, and when there's tension within them, our entire emotional foundation feels shaken.

It's one thing to manage our own feelings, but when we throw in the variable of another person's unpredictable, always-changing emotions, even the healthiest relationships can leave us disappointed and depressed at times. Here's how my friend and fellow podcaster Tony Miltenberger describes this phenomenon: "Marriage and parenting have the potential for such emotional intensity because inside these relationships are two people bumping into each other's wounds."[1]

We have to discern not only what we're feeling below the surface but we must also understand what tricky emotions the other person is facing. We must balance logic and emotion inside ourselves while giving space for someone else to wrestle with this internal turmoil. And we're called to respond in kindness, even if we feel anything but. All with the goal of making both parties feel understood and restoring peace to the relationship.

You know, *simple stuff*.

So where do we start? How do we navigate the world of not only our emotions but also the emotions of someone we have no control over?

It Starts and Ends with Love

The Beatles claimed that "all you need is love," and to some extent, I have to agree. Let's just decide to love each other and all our emotional frustrations will be solved, right? The timeless song did leave out a few essential details though, such as *how* to love when all we want to do is . . . well, *hate*. You know, when all those "emotional wounds" keep bumping into each other.

That's a bit more complex, right? Let's start with the ADD principles as our guide for how to choose to love.

First, love honors both sides of the argument (acknowledge). Loving others through emotional tension starts with using empathy to acknowledge why the other person's frustrations make sense. At the same time, love is not ignorant to our own hurts because God is not ignorant to our hurts. We must compassionately bring our own pain to the light so God can heal it too.

Second, love seeks wisdom and truth despite heightened feelings (discern). God's truth is unchanging, but oh how our personal perceptions can influence our interpretation of a situation! Love stands in the other person's shoes and asks, *How are* you *seeing this?* It also identifies lies and half-truths with gentleness and respect as the Bible instructs (Eph. 4:15; 1 Pet. 3:15–16).

Third, love takes action to heal the relationship and to honor God (decide). While we all long to be the *recipients* of love, we're foremost called to be *instigators*. Love is the source of forgiveness and patient endurance through relationship frustrations. It takes action toward relationship restoration and should be given whether or not others meet our emotional needs.

Speaking of having a loving attitude, one of the greatest things about love is that we don't have to muster it up. Love comes from God, and we can ask for His love for others to flow through us (1 John 4:7–8).

God *can* help us supernaturally love others when we don't feel loving, but He *can't* make us choose to love. We get to decide if we will be loving or not. We are not responsible for whether or not the other person will be loving, and that can be heartbreaking to accept. Sometimes we have to set healthy boundaries in the relationship if it's not safe to explore emotions together. At the end of the day, however, we will individually answer to God for our actions, and He will ask, *Did you love others like I loved you?*

If you need help choosing to love someone despite your emotional pain, download the "I Choose to Love" audio declaration found at the link at the end of this chapter. This is a great statement to listen to on repeat when you're battling relationship tension.

Let's dial this down further. How can we use the ADD principles to manage emotions as we choose to love others through everyday relationship conflict?

Applying ADD to Relationship Conflicts

Scripture gives us three healthy ways to deal with relationship frustrations: (1) ask God for wisdom on how to process what we're feeling (James 1:5); (2) ask God for wisdom on how to approach that person (Ps. 5:8; 25:4; 143:8); and (3) release the emotional frustration to Him and forgive the other person for what happened (2 Cor. 2:7, 10; 12:13).

We need to go to God about our emotions first before speaking to the other person as it may be something we can resolve just with His help (more on that later on). If we're called to share our feelings with others, here are some practical ways to guide the conversation.

Acknowledge

First, notice the emotions that are present. Take a moment to see what's going on inside yourself, noticing why that makes sense and what compassion God offers for any internal frustrations. Does this need to be talked through with God before inviting the other person into the conversation? What surface-level emotions might be present, such as anger or sadness? Are there any secondary emotions that can be identified?

Next, consider what the other person might be feeling. What words, body language, and other cues give insight as to what's going on inside of them? Anger and general frustration can be obvious outward emotions, but remember that these may be just the surface-level feelings. Depending on how familiar you are with the person and the situation, it may be possible to surmise some of the person's other secondary emotions. What makes these feelings reasonable for them?

After that, consider how to offer empathy for what they're experiencing, such as physically reassuring them with a touch or verbally acknowledging their frustrated emotional state in a way that feels appropriate. If it makes sense to proceed with a conversation, ask the other person for a reasonable time to talk. Whether before, during, or after a conversation, allow space to process or time to calm down if either of you need it.

Once the conversation progresses and you are able to discuss the facts of the situation, allow them to express what they're feeling at their own pace. While we can't force emotional expression from someone else, we can acknowledge what they *are* expressing without offering judgment. Reflect back what they share with statements like "it sounds like you're feeling [X emotion]" or "it makes sense you're feeling [X emotion] because of [Y situation]." Compassionately acknowledging others' pain points helps them to feel seen and heard, a critical piece of building trust that also eases emotional reconciliation.

As it feels safe and appropriate, share feelings using phrases like "I'm feeling [X emotion] because of [Y situation]." Notice how the other person responds to what you say. If they show empathy and a willingness to listen, express why the feelings make sense. Ideally, they can reflect those feelings back to indicate that the feelings are important and valid.

Discern

You can invite discernment into the conversation as it seems appropriate and nonthreatening to both parties. Consider what truth can be identified about this situation. What lies need to be admitted? Is either person processing this situation through certain filters such as past hurts or fears? What's God's perspective on the circumstance?

Try to stay calm at every point in the conversation. Remember, it's okay to take a breather for a few minutes or to use emotional prep tools if things become too painful to proceed or if either party needs a minute to process. We can't control how someone else views a situation, even if what's true seems painfully obvious to us, so leave space for the other person's viewpoint. Stay soft to their pain. Any hard-to-process truths that are shared should be viewed through the lens of Christ's love.

If it feels safe to do so, consider talking about how this situation may be related to other past or present pain for either person. Continue to use the tools of empathy and reflective statements such as "wow, I can understand why you feel [X emotion] based on what you just shared" or "I've felt that way too."

In addition, choose to view the circumstances with vulnerability over victimhood when facing frustrations about others. His or her emotional pain may have nothing to do with you; likewise, the pain you feel may be ultimately unrelated to the person across from you. Try to see the truth from both sides and to understand how the heightened emotions may be about a lot more than this singular situation. If the other person is a Christian, share any encouraging or helpful biblical truths as you feel led, always in the spirit of love and respect.

Decide

Once both parties have had a chance to acknowledge their feelings and some truths and lies about the situation have come to light through discernment, consider some alternatives for how to find resolution. What do both people need in order to feel released from these difficult emotions? How might each person be able to help the other find emotional healing?

Respond to any conviction the Holy Spirit may be offering, and as needed, confess any sins or misunderstandings. We can't demand confession or repentance from others. But if it feels safe, we can tell someone else if we were hurt by their actions and then leave the next steps up to God. Sometimes the other person knows they are the cause of the pain, but they may not be able to come to terms with that yet. In these moments we can ask for God's help to remain loving and kind. Although, depending on the circumstances, it may be wise to establish some relationship boundaries until the connection is fully rectified.

What other steps may God be calling both parties to take? Consider if this situation requires further action beyond this conversation for resolution. Should this issue be discussed more in the future, or does it seem resolved? If additional processing is required, would it be helpful to include a third party to help both of you process your feelings more effectively?

See if any frustrations are still present and determine what aspects of that are in your control. Is there anything you need to surrender to God? What fears or worries need to be yielded to His control?

Last, take a moment to determine where to emotionally dwell as a result of this interaction. For example, is more time required to process the feelings? If trust was broken, is it wise for each person to be more wary in their future interactions? Did this situation reveal other relationship frustrations that might need to be processed or released? How can each person reset their emotions by focusing on praise? Each person can choose to help his or her mind rest in quiet confidence by using a statement like "I will choose to adopt [X mindset] when I'm feeling upset about this issue."

Again, there's no perfect template for having a healthy conversation when heated emotions are involved. Use the principles of *acknowledge*, *discern*, and *decide* in a way that feels natural and advantageous in your situation.

It can also be helpful to have some established ground rules for processing emotions in relationships, especially in close connections like marriage where loving conversation through emotions is a mainstay. Download the "10 Ground Rules for Processing Emotions in Relationships" found at the link at the end of the chapter.

Using ADD When You Disagree

Why does the call to love others seem to fly out the window when someone shares a different political ideology or worldview? Whether on social media or in real life, we've all seen how intense emotions rooted in strong opinions can quickly turn a civil conversation into a nasty and mean confrontation.

Emotions don't have to be our guide as we determine how to respond to those with different opinions. We must respect others, being careful not to label any issue as "black or white" outside of what God has determined in His Word. Respect doesn't require agreement, just a recognition that both people are humans created in the image of God.

Believe it or not, the Bible gives each person the right to believe what they want to believe, even if their views are in opposition to God's truth. Romans 1 tells us that God makes His truth plain to everyone, but each person decides whether or not to follow Him and live by His laws. He offers this choice with kindness and respect and does not force us to change but woos us to His ways. We can give others the same courtesy when we encounter their differing opinions.

We are called to point out evil from good and to stand up for justice, but there is a time to be silent and a time to speak up (Eccles. 3:7). It's not our job to convince others of our opinions, ultimately. We are each responsible for our own viewpoints, and we can leave the results of those opinions in God's capable hands as the ultimate judge of the universe.

We don't have to agree with others, but we still must treat them with love. No matter how emotionally charged up the verbal exchange, there's no excuse for name-calling, slander, or hate speech. Even if we're on opposite ends of an issue, we can use a tool like ADD to bring compassion, clarity, and loving action to the discussion. Here's how:

Acknowledge: Recognize the other person's opinion on the topic. Chances are good that you're probably already well-versed with your own opinion, so consider the other person's biggest grievances. If possible, ask them to share their stance on the issue and verbally reflect it back in a respectful manner.

Discern: Better understand their viewpoint. If you are comfortable, see if they are willing to share how they developed their stance on a certain subject. Notice how their background, cultural heritage, neighborhood, financial status, trauma, spiritual beliefs, and other influences have affected how they perceive the issue. Listen with an open mind and ask God for insight and understanding. Yes, it can be hard to hear someone else's thoughts when they seem diametrically opposed to our own, but we must remember that we live in a highly divisive culture strengthened by algorithm-driven social media feeds meant to keep us locked in our own ideological bubbles. While we are uniquely influenced by our surroundings and experiences, we are all created by God and therefore deserve to be treated with kindness and respect.

Decide: Determine how the Holy Spirit may want you to respond in love. God may call you to gently speak His truth over them, to share your opposing perspective, or even to witness about Christ as part of the conversation. Or He may encourage you to keep your mouth shut and simply listen—a lost skill in a culture that praises those with the loudest voices. Maybe God will reveal that a disagreement about this issue isn't a deal-breaker for the relationship, or perhaps it is. Maybe this person's opinion will change your views on the topic (hey, it could happen). No matter your response, act in love and under God's direction.

Reconciliation isn't always possible when opinions differ, but we can still choose kindness and understanding even in the heat of inflamed, fiery emotions. Soft words cloaked in love and respect strengthen an argument much more than ones spoken in anger and rage. If you're finding it hard to speak respectfully to someone with an opposing viewpoint, step away from the conversation, use emotional prep tools to calm your spirit, and ask God for help.

When It Doesn't Feel Safe to Share

What do we do with big emotions toward others when we can't speak to that person about how we're feeling? They may be emotionally closed off or they may have passed on. Perhaps it feels threatening to share with this person, especially if there is emotional baggage from previous situations. We all know people who use passive aggression or manipulation to not-so-subtly communicate their feelings, which certainly doesn't make us want to bare our souls.

Some of us have inner soundtracks that hinder our ability to share our emotions. We may not want to "upset" others with our emotions—a common issue for people pleasers. For those who struggle with perfectionism or performance-as-worth mindsets, it can feel scary to share feelings with anyone because of a negative connotation of emotions being "bad" or a sign of weakness.

Others of us were punished for having difficult or out-of-control emotions, and this has taught us to hide our feelings and plaster on a smile. Cassidy, a member of my Christian Mindset Makeover program, said that she has a hard time showing emotions, especially when she's feeling sad and disappointed. "It wasn't safe for me to cry when I was little without getting into trouble," she shared. "Now I struggle with finding emotional boundaries and knowing when it's safe to let out my feelings."

Past statements from others like "you're being ridiculous," "stop being so upset about that," or "get control of yourself" can echo in our heads for years and cause us to keep our emotions locked up tight. As a child, one of my coaching clients Sophia was repeatedly told that her emotions made her "soft and weak." For years this imprinting not only forced her to keep her emotions locked away but also fed her need to please others and to micromanage every detail of her family's life. "I like to be in control and to keep everyone happy with my actions. Being vulnerable with my feelings makes me feel weak and threatened. What if my family members are no longer happy with me when I share what's inside?"

Like with acknowledging our feelings, sharing them also requires vulnerability, and vulnerability always comes with a potential loss of control. Being emotionally naked in front of someone can be terrifying, especially if we've shared with others and were misunderstood or wounded because of our transparency.

If you can relate to any of this, please know that you're not alone. I still sometimes struggle with an ability to share my emotions freely in my closest relationships because I'm afraid I will somehow disappoint the other person or that I will lose their love. As a young adult I used to overshare to create a sense of closeness with others, but I also went through a season where I was burned so badly by sharing with others that I turned away from pursuing close relationships altogether. Through trial and error, I've had to learn when it's safe to share and when it's not.

The good news is that we don't have to have the same emotional boundaries with everyone. It is a precious gift, indeed, to reveal our truest selves to someone else. Others earn our emotional trust, and we earn theirs. Vulnerability and safety take time to build in relationships, and frankly, not every person we encounter has cultivated the emotional collateral required for the deepest levels of sharing. It's heartbreaking to admit but some people can never be trusted with our deepest feelings, even if we've known them for years and desperately long for that connection with them. We don't have to feel guilty for creating emotional boundaries with those who haven't earned our trust or made us feel emotionally safe.

In addition, God is committed to heal those broken places in us where we've been emotionally wounded. Even if others continue to hurt us, we have the promise of God's unfailing love as a steady anchor for our souls (Rom. 8:39). If we've experienced trauma, we can ask God for help in discerning when to share and with whom to give our emotional trust.

Even if we can't fully express ourselves to certain people, we can share our hurts with God. He helps us relate to our emotional selves in new ways, reminding us that even if we feel judged and misunderstood by everyone else, our feelings are never "too much" for Him to handle. He knows everything we feel and loves us through every up-and-down emotion (Ps. 139:1–6). As we deepen our fellowship with Him, our emotional trust in Him also deepens, giving us a new resilience for managing difficult feelings in a healthy way.

Like in any relationship, building trust with God takes time, so be patient with yourself if you aren't sure that you can trust God with your emotions. He is always a gentleman and is never in a rush. He will prove Himself faithful as you become ready to give Him room in your heart.

Using ADD to Prepare Ourselves for Emotional Triggers

We all have certain situations or specific people that are instant emotional triggers. From big traumas to tiny annoyances, quite often these encounters are unavoidable, and many happen over and over again. (You know, like that obnoxious mom from the soccer team who won't stop boasting about her son's otherworldly athletic abilities and perfect test scores.) If we can't avoid or resolve these situations, we can use ADD to prepare ourselves for when they pop up.

Acknowledge: Prepare yourself by predicting what might set you off. When we anticipate an emotionally triggering situation, we're using our brain's foreknowledge and estimation skills to help us avoid future pain. While we don't need to let our amygdala's what-if questions take over so we're swirling in anxiety, we can soften the emotional blow of tricky situations by simply acknowledging that they are possible. For example, as we walk into a meeting with a notoriously difficult client, we can tell ourselves, *This guy is known for having a dismissive and gruff demeanor. If he becomes grouchy, remember it's probably not about me.*

Discern: Remind yourself about what is true and not true about this trigger and any related situations. Reaffirming truth is another excellent strategy. Clearly identifying truth from lies before the encounter is like putting on battle armor for the enemy's arrows.

Using ADD as a People Pleaser

Does your desire to make others happy and to keep the peace some-times make it hard to have healthy emotional responses? Try using ADD to work through a tendency to people-please.

First, **acknowledge** why it's hard to say no to this person or why you're tempted to placate their needs in an unhealthy way. For ex-ample, ask yourself, Why does it make sense that I want this person to be happy with me?

Next, **discern** what's true and what's not true so lies can be clearly seen. Ask, What is God calling me to do? What is the truth about this situation or about how I'm feeling? Am I afraid of disappointing this person, and if so, why?

Last, **decide** what the healthiest alternative is and where you'll emotionally dwell. Consider a statement like, "I've decided to move forward because God has called me to do this, even if others may be upset. I can trust God's guidance, and I choose to let go of any fear of man or need to defend myself."

These can be simple statements we agree to use as a filter should we be triggered by the other person, such as: "I may not like his behavior, but I'm not responsible for it," "I don't have to choose to see reality the way she does," or "Even if he hasn't chosen to move on in this area, I can still move on."

Decide: Be willing to allow any potential triggers to build emotional resilience. Once we recognize a potential emotional pitfall and can discern the situation's truth from lies, we can decide how to respond and where to emotionally dwell. For instance, we can say: "I can choose to let this person trigger me or not. I'm decid-ing not to let him trigger me." We can even put together some contingency plans should our emotions get the best of us, such as, "If she starts complaining about her husband again, I'm going to excuse myself to the bathroom." We can also plan ahead and decide to let God guide us. Here's an example statement we can repeat internally: "I've talked to God about this person's behavior and asked for His help. I will stay calm and believe that He will give me everything I need to respond in the moment."

By now we've seen that ADD is a highly versatile emotional management tool that can be used in many ways. But did you know that there are habits we can build to make ADD an easier, more natural process? Let's talk about that in our final chapter.

CHAPTER QUESTIONS

1. What were some of your biggest takeaways from this chapter?
2. Which relationships or life situations would most benefit from the tools shared in this chapter?
3. Which tools or concepts will you experiment with when it comes to managing emotions in relationships?
4. What are some emotional triggers that you can prepare yourself for? How will you emotionally prepare yourself based on what you learned?

Testimonial

I used to really struggle with ruminating on negative thoughts. If a friend said something hurtful, it would consume my mind for days. But ADD has been a game changer for my thought life. Now I can lovingly examine my thoughts and say, "It's okay that I'm feeling hurt or feeling rejected."

ADD has given me permission and courage to be honest with other people too. I can tell them, "That was hurtful, and I'm processing what you said." As a result, my emotions aren't nearly so up and down, and I've seen a big change in my relationships.

Caroline, coaching client

Don't forget to check out the free downloads for
Emotional Confidence! There's a quiz, helpful exercises,
and even audio and video tools to help you continue
your journey in managing your emotions.

Go to AliciaMichelle.com/Emotional-Downloads
to access these free resources.

17

Habits and Next Steps for Ongoing Emotional Confidence

Have you ever tried pushing a wheelbarrow uphill with a flat tire? Or pedaling a bike that's been left outside in the rain to rust? The wheelbarrow and the bike may move, but it takes a ton of extra effort because we're working against the flat tire and the rust. We must remove the obstacle or fix broken areas (such as adding air to a tire) for optimum performance.

ADD is kind of like that. It becomes a lot easier to use when we build in ongoing mental health supports that "grease the gears."

13 Habits That Make It Easier to Build Emotional Confidence

In our final chapter, let's talk about some simple habits that make managing emotions with ADD easier as we cultivate emotional confidence.

Note: You may notice similarities between this list and the emotional prep tools in chapter 4. That's because these concepts are helpful in both high-stress moments as well as regular practices.

1. Lean into emotional confidence–building opportunities. Life gives us tons of opportunities for our feelings to go haywire, unfortunately. The good news is these can be awesome chances to practice ADD. Every good athlete or musician knows that they must spend hours practicing in order for their skills to become natural and for their confidence to build. In those moments when we're confronted with something challenging—again—we can take a deep breath and ask God for a good attitude as we get our ADD "reps" in.

2. Rest in God when processing challenging emotions. It can be tempting to run from what we're feeling or to stuff down our emotions, especially if that's how we've always handled them. It takes courage to turn toward emotional processing. Thankfully God is our comforter and safe haven in these moments. When the Israelites were freaking out as they found themselves backed up against the Red Sea while being pursued by the Egyptians, God told them to stay calm and let Him rescue them (Exod. 14:10–14). In the same way, we can choose to stay calm and let God do the healing work in us as we say yes to processing emotions.

3. Regularly check in with the emotional self. In chapter 6 we talked about how the practice of morning pages—writing three pages of whatever is on your mind each day—is a great emotional acknowledgment tool, especially when we're processing lots of big feelings. Even just spending a few minutes a week journaling a response to a question like "How am I doing emotionally?" can do wonders for ongoing emotional management. Doing a daily or weekly check-in with our emotional selves in each area of life sweeps away any mental cobwebs that have built up.

4. Slow down and make space for Sabbath. Living a rushed, hectic life makes it that much harder to have patience with ourselves as we process our emotions, and it is extremely difficult to stay in step with the slow, gentle pace of Jesus. When we're overscheduled and worn-out, we turn to the fast-food version of dealing with our feelings: pushing them down, distracting ourselves from the pain, or letting our feelings fly unchecked and unbridled. We desperately need Jesus's whispers of empathy and wisdom to ground us when our feelings are out of control, and healthy boundaries in our schedules make room for His loving counsel.

5. Choose to mentally dwell in God's love regularly. I had a light bulb moment in my spiritual and emotional wellness journey when I discovered that I could regularly calm myself by meditating on how much God loved me. At first this felt weirdly self-indulgent and needy, like I was an insecure girlfriend who needed reassurance that, yes, I am pretty. But I quickly realized that when I regularly soaked my soul in the truth that I was loved, it became second nature to acknowledge my painful emotions with compassion instead of criticism. God's loving heartbeat for my challenges grew louder than the inner critic's bleating tones, and this brought so much freedom! He *cares* for us, friend! He *walks with us* in pain! He *redeems* our tragedies. Oh, may those sentiments change our perceptions and may our ears never grow tired of hearing them.

6. Fill the mind with God's clarifying voice of truth daily. We can't know what God would say in the *discern* step if we aren't regularly refocusing our minds on His wisdom. We're immersed in a culture that constantly bombards us with false messages about our identity, so we must counterbalance that onslaught with the purifying reality of God's wisdom that can be found only in Scripture. Whether it's a formal Bible study or a commitment to read the Bible and respond each day in a journal, this daily spiritual cleansing is a must for building emotional confidence.

7. Practice ongoing surrender to God in all things. God makes room for our questions, but a rich sense of peace settles in our spirits when we choose to stop asking why and simply obey. When we've cultivated this habit of surrendered obedience, it becomes so much easier to courageously follow God's direction when we move into the *decide* step. When we practice listening to God's voice and obeying His leadership—even when our questions are not answered—we not only grow in closeness to Him but share in His blessings and wisdom (Lev. 26:3–13; Exod. 19:5–6; Prov. 2:11).

8. Create other habits that build a positive mental attitude. We don't need to pretend that life is perfect, but when we develop simple practices that acknowledge the hard but emotionally dwell in the good, we can live in a more positive emotional equilibrium overall. This doesn't have to be fancy or complicated. For example, it can be as simple as a daily or weekly gratitude practice.

Since it's easy for gratitude to feel forced or stale when it becomes routine, I like to reframe it as actively looking for God's fingerprints in every area of life. We can see Him in a beautiful sunset, an unexpected encounter with a friend, a great deal on a new outfit—the sky is the limit! I think of these as little touches from heaven reminding me that my heavenly Father is always actively at work in my life, and they help me keep my heart focused on praise instead of self-pity when my emotions are all over the place.

9. Counter the heaviness of difficult emotions with laughter, fun, and play. Maybe it sounds strange, but as someone with a type A personality, I have had to learn how to have fun. I schedule free time in my calendar for activities that fill my soul and bring me joy, such as drawing and watercolor painting, exploring new areas of the city, and quality time with loved ones.

I'm also learning how to laugh more and not take everything so seriously, and I have my sister Kris to thank for that. She is one of the funniest people I know and can make me pee-in-my-pants laugh like no one else! Regularly connect with life-giving people and fun activities that renew your emotional energy, especially during tough seasons.

10. Get a good night's sleep. A fascinating study on the connection between sleep and emotional wellness demonstrated that just one sleepless night makes us more emotionally fragile and can trigger a "robust spike in anxiety and depression the following morning."[1] Another study credits high-quality sleep as one effective coping strategy to counteract the increased risk of depression and anxiety as a result of chronic stress.[2]

Why do our sleep habits so greatly affect our emotional health? One theory is that the activity of the prefrontal cortex, the logical center of the brain that helps dampen the amygdala's emotional "freak-out" reaction to stress, decreases drastically when sleep is disrupted. In addition, MRIs show that the neural connection between the prefrontal cortex and the amygdala becomes significantly weaker when we get less sleep.[3] While some argue that too much sleep can have adverse effects, aiming for an average of eight hours a night of sleep is a powerful way to enrich our brain's ability to stay emotionally centered.

11. Eat to balance blood sugar and to support gut health and overall nutrition. The brain runs mainly on glucose, a type of sugar we get from food, and low or highly fluctuating glucose levels can have a dramatic impact on our moods.[4] There's also a growing body of research that connects mental health with gut health. Scientists have discovered that the *enteric nervous system*, a network of more than one hundred million nerve cells that line the gastrointestinal tract, communicates directly with our brain, and can greatly affect our emotional responses.[5] Other studies show that eating overly processed foods may increase depression, and that those who ate more fruits and vegetables had a lower depression risk and a better sense of well-being.[6] Just one more reason to focus on a healthy diet and watch our sugar intake, right?

12. Consider how fluctuating hormones affect emotions in your current life stage. It's no secret that hormones greatly influence a woman's emotional well-being, not only during her menstrual cycle but throughout every reproductive stage, including puberty, postpartum, and perimenopause.[7] When hormone levels drop during times like perimenopause, serotonin—the "feel good" neurotransmitter—also drops, which contributes to increased sadness, irritability, and mood swings.[8] Along with affecting basic body rhythms like sleep, these hormonal dips can make it harder to roll with life's punches or can even trigger depression. Some signs of a hormonal imbalance include irregular menstruation, hot flashes, and unexplained weight gain or loss.[9] Check with your doctor to determine if any emotional ups and downs you're experiencing could be related to hormonal imbalance. Men also face hormonal changes that can affect mood.

13. Incorporate exercise into your routine. Exercise, which I like to call *joyful movement*, brings an instant boost to our mental health. Whether it's due to the increase in blood flow to the brain, the release of happiness-inducing neurotransmitters like dopamine, or other factors, exercise is proven to reduce anxiety, depression, and negative moods.[10] Researchers at the University of South Australia found that physical activity is one and a half times more effective in treating depression than psychotherapy or antidepressants![11] And good news: experts say that just thirty minutes of moderately intense exercise three days a week is enough to see exercise's mental health benefits.[12] I definitely see a consistent correlation between the quality of my attitude and the amount I've exercised each week.

Final Encouragements for Building a Lifestyle of Emotional Confidence

Emotional confidence is a skill we'll build our entire lives, and we have God's permission to learn and grow imperfectly. We can stop rating our emotional confidence as "good" or "bad" at each stage but instead, see each opportunity to manage our feelings as learning moments on a path toward holiness and sanctification. Even when we're equipped with tools like ADD, we're not going to stop having challenging emotions, so we can't expect ourselves to "arrive" on this journey or to always manage our volatile feelings flawlessly.

Never forget that emotions are a gift from God to help us better understand ourselves and our world. We are relational creatures, and emotions are a primary way we build life-giving connections with others, with ourselves, and with Him. Let's keep noticing the emotions inside, listening to His wisdom to separate truth from lies, and bravely following the Holy Spirit's lead as we live for His glory!

CHAPTER QUESTIONS

1. What feels like your biggest obstacle to processing emotions on a regular basis?
2. Which of these habits do you currently practice?
3. Which of these habits will you experiment with to see how they affect your emotional confidence?
4. What's the next step for you in your emotional management journey?

Testimonial

ADD becomes easier when I'm taking good care of myself. I decided to get serious about my mental health, and that included setting myself up for success by going to bed earlier, taking a walk each morning, and laying off the sweets. It's been a process, but I've been so encouraged by how these little changes in my habits really make it easier to use ADD, and in turn, make my emotions feel less out of control. Whoa, what a difference that's made in my life!

Alison, coaching client

Don't forget to check out the free downloads for *Emotional Confidence*! There's a quiz, helpful exercises, and even audio and video tools to help you continue your journey in managing your emotions.

Go to AliciaMichelle.com/Emotional-Downloads to access these free resources.

Acknowledgments

God has used many puzzle pieces to shape me into who I am today as an author, coach, and podcaster, and it's taken an army of unseen others over the years to shape the thoughts behind the words in this book. This is my feeble attempt to recognize a few of those people.

First, thank you to my agent Keely whose professionalism and knowledge were my backbone, especially as we were shopping this title. Thank you to all the wonderful staff at Baker Publishing Group—the editing, design, and marketing teams—who caught this book's vision from day one. Thank you to my launch team manager Sarah whose friendship and expertise made this process even more fun. I'm so appreciative of the hours each of you has spent pouring into this project. Thank you!

To the amazing people who make my daily life so much easier: my assistant Ally, my podcast team, and my video editor Erick. You are wonderful to work with, and I'm so grateful for you!

Many thanks to my professors and mentor coaches over the years, including those from the Missouri School of Journalism ("trim the fat!") and the Professional Christian Coaching Institute ("don't get hooked!"). Thank you to my business coaches who've helped me dream big and create plans to make those dreams a reality. (PS: I did it! I wrote a book!)

Thank you to Nikki, the college student who stood at the door of the student ministry meeting and befriended me when I knew no one, including Christ. For three years, you faithfully answered my (many) God questions, loved me when I didn't love myself, and quietly modeled what it means to be a dedicated, sold-out woman of God. There's no way I could have written a book on inviting God into our emotions if you hadn't introduced me to Him all those years ago. May I have the opportunity to impact others the way you've impacted me.

Thank you to my friend Sandy who poured into this weary, disillusioned young mom all those years ago with her overwhelming kindness and love. I still think about our morning walks where you taught me all the flower names and how we'd sit outside and watch little R chase the butterflies. You taught me how to be gentle with myself and to stop and savor life over a spot of tea, and that's dramatically changed my life and my ability to manage my emotions.

For all the wonderful men and women who have officially and unofficially invested in my spiritual and emotional growth: you gave me permission to feel my feelings and bring them before our loving God. Thank you for listening to my fears, wiping my tears, and reminding me of God's steadfast presence. From the MOPS moms in those early years, to women's Bible study friends, to my Bloom ladies—wow, I'm so blessed to laugh, love, grow, worship, pray, and serve God beside you. Thank you for your prayers and encouragement as I ran my book marathon. I treasure each of you!

To our incredible life group: your vulnerability, generosity, and laughter make life group my favorite way to spend a Wednesday night! Thank you for covering every stage of this book journey with prayer and encouragement. Lisa, thank you for your willingness to read through those first rough pages and for offering priceless feedback! And, Scott, I must admit—it is impossible to quantify the depth of your contribution to this book.

Thank you to my podcasting, coaching, and writing friends who have supported me through every step of this book journey. You inspire me and bless me with your kindness! Carlie, the words of life you've spoken over me have made a dramatic difference.

Because of you, I'm still "thanking God in advance" for the good things to come.

Thank you to *The Christian Mindset Coach* podcast listeners and everyone in my online community. I pray this book inspires you to better connect with Jesus as you grow in emotional confidence and better understand His immense love for you.

Many thanks to the ladies from my coaching practice and in the Christian Mindset Makeover. Your vulnerability is beautiful and teaches me so much about managing emotions in the real world. I'm incredibly honored to witness God's transforming work in your life. You are each such radiant, vibrant women of God poised to make great impact for the kingdom. I treasure you! I'm always "with you and for you"!

Much love and thanks to my parents who have known me and cared for me from the start! Dad, thank you for always encouraging me to write (see, I'm using my degree) and for being an example of a man committed to his job and to his family. Mom, thank you for always being there to listen and for sharing your kindness and love. I love you both very much!

Grandma and Grandpa, I'm thankful to have known you, and I miss you every single day. Grandpa, your laughter could fill a room, and your wisdom could fill a shelfful of books. Grandma, your comforting hugs made me feel seen, and your hilarious comments (about everyone and everything) kept me in stitches. I can't wait to hug you both in heaven.

Thank you to my in-laws and extended family on my husband's side. Dad, thank you for your quiet, steadfast example. Mom, thank you for your fierce hugs and passionate heart that was so on fire for Christ. I will always tell the story of how your prayers brought your son and me together! Christina, you are a selfless, wonderful woman of God, and I cherish the memories from our trip down the coast.

I am so grateful for my sister Kris and her family. Jesus, thank You for healing our relationship! Kris, I look at you and am in awe of all that you've conquered and of what a gift you are to this world. And yes, you are the funniest person I know, B! Here's to more weird photos, inside jokes, and chances to say "pretty good, pretty good" together!

To my children and (someday) grandchildren: your patience, grace, and laughter as we discover how to love each other through every season is a priceless gift. Words can't express how much I love each of you. May you always follow Christ and know the joy of having a deep relationship with our Savior. He will be there to love you through tears of joy and sadness. Lean on God for compassion, clarity, and courage as He helps you better understand your feelings. Your dad and I are always in your corner.

To the one person who knows all my emotional highs and lows better than anyone, my incredible husband: we've walked through so much together, and you have been that steady beacon of calm through it all. Even though your lack of outward emotions drives me crazy sometimes ("I *am* ecstatic, Alicia. Can't you tell?") I know that God made you to be my perfect complement. Thank you for asking me to marry you (even though I almost botched the whole thing), for being the finder of all lost things in our house, and for continuing to faithfully love me for over twenty-three years. When we keep our eyes on Jesus, we can do anything together. You are and will always be my best friend.

And to Jesus, the almighty King of the universe and Savior of my soul. You deserve the highest praise for anything and everything good in my life. Thank You for teaching me to love myself the way You love me, flaws and all. I'm so grateful for this life You've given me. Every earthly treasure pales in comparison to the gift of knowing You. May everything I do be by Your strength and for Your eternal glory.

Notes

Chapter 1 The Cost of Hiding, Stuffing, and Running from Our Emotions

1. Kate Bowler, *No Cure for Being Human and Other Truths I Need to Hear* (New York: Penguin Random House, 2021), 15–18.

2. The doctors who helped with my case never gave a definitive cause for my vertebral artery dissections. These kinds of injuries typically happen to those who've endured physical trauma to the arteries from a sudden violent event involving the neck, such as a car accident. As I explored the potential causes for my injury, I ran across several studies that spoke of how high levels of stress, specifically a steady drip of hormones like cortisol, could break down internal tissue and cause injuries to soft tissues like blood vessels.

3. Jennifer Michalowski, "How the Brain Balances Pleasure and Pain," Cold Spring Harbor Laboratory, December 31, 2019, https://www.cshl.edu/how-the-brain-balances-pleasure-and-pain/.

4. Kristina Robb-Dover, "How Negative Emotions Affect Health," FHE Health, June 12, 2020, https://fherehab.com/learning/negative-emotions-health.

5. "COVID-19 Pandemic Triggers 25% Increase in Prevalence of Anxiety and Depression Worldwide," World Health Organization, March 2, 2022, https://www.who.int/news/item/02-03-2022-covid-19-pandemic-triggers-25-increase-in-prevalence-of-anxiety-and-depression-worldwide.

6. "Percentage of Respondents in the U.S. who Reported Symptoms of Depressive Disorder in the Last Seven Days or Two Weeks from April 2020 to August 2023, by Gender," Statista, accessed February 1, 2024, https://www.statista.com/statistics/1132653/depressive-symptoms-us-adults-by-gender-past-week/.

7. "Quit Your Stinkin' Thinkin,'" Facebook video, posted by Joyce Meyer Ministries, September 4, 2017, https://www.facebook.com/watch/?v=10155840283982384.

8. Maanvi Singh, "If You Feel Thankful, Write It Down. It's Good for Your Health," NPR, December 24, 2018, https://www.npr.org/sections/health-shots/2018/12/24/678232331/if-you-feel-thankful-write-it-down-its-good-for-your-health.

9. Bowler, *No Cure for Being Human*, 20.

10. U.S. Surgeon General, "Our Epidemic of Loneliness and Isolation," U.S. Public Health Services, May 2, 2023, https://www.hhs.gov/sites/default/files/surgeon-general-social-connection-advisory.pdf.

11. Stephane Cote, Anett Gyurak, and Robert W. Levinson, "The Ability to Regulate Emotion Is Associated with Greater Well-Being, Income, and Socioeconomic Status," *American Psychological Association* 10, no, 6 (2010): 922–23, https://psycnet.apa.org/record/2010-25761-009.

12. Brené Brown, *Dare to Lead: Daring Greatly and Rising Strong at Work* (London: Penguin Random House, 2018), 146–47.

13. John P. Rafferty, "Thorndike's Law of Effect," Britannica, accessed February 12, 2024, https://www.britannica.com/science/Thorndikes-law-of-effect.

Chapter 2 Understanding and Defining Emotions

1. *APA Dictionary of Psychology*, s.v. "emotion," https://dictionary.apa.org/emotion.

2. Goran Simic et al., "Understanding Emotions: Origins and Roles of the Amygdala," *Biomolecules* 11, no. 6 (2021), https://www.mdpi.com/2218-273X/11/6/823.

3. Elizabeth Scott, "What Is a Highly Sensitive Person (HSP)?," *Verywell Mind*, June 13, 2023, https://www.verywellmind.com/highly-sensitive-persons-traits-that-create-more-stress-4126393.

4. Shahram Heshmat, "Why Do We Remember Certain Things, but Forget Others?," *Psychology Today*, October 8, 2015, https://www.psychologytoday.com/us/blog/science-choice/201510/why-do-we-remember-certain-things-forget-others.

5. Kendra Cherry, "Emotions and Types of Emotional Responses," *Verywell Mind*, June 29, 2023, https://www.verywellmind.com/what-are-emotions-2795178.

6. Lauri Nummenmaa, Enrico Glerean, and Ritta Hari, "Bodily Maps of Emotions," *PNAS* 111, no. 2 (2013): 646–51, https://www.pnas.org/doi/10.1073/pnas.1321664111.

7. Universität Basel, "Men and Women Process Emotions Differently," Science Daily, January 20, 2015, https://www.sciencedaily.com/releases/2015/01/150120185853.htm.

8. Philippe Verduyn and Sakia Lavrijsen, "Which Emotions Last Longest and Why: The Role of Event Importance and Rumination," *Motivation and Emotion* 39 (October 2014): 119–27, https://doi.org/10.1007/s11031-014-9445-y.

9. "Why Are Teens Girls Suffering from Record Levels of Sadness and Suicidality?," Amen Clinics, April 25, 2023, https://www.amenclinics.com/blog/why-are-teen-girls-suffering-from-record-levels-of-sadness-and-suicidality.

10. Sarah Whittle, Julian G. Simmons, and Nicholas B. Allen, "Emotion and Gender-Specific Neural Processing in Men and Women," in *Principles of Gender-Specific Medicine*, 3rd ed., (Cambridge, MA: Academic Press, 2017), 183–201.

11. Neel Burton, "What Are Basic Emotions?," *Psychology Today*, October 21, 2022, https://www.psychologytoday.com/us/blog/hide-and-seek/201601/what-are-basic-emotions.

12. University of West Alabama, "The Science of Emotion: Exploring the Basics of Emotional Psychology," Psychology and Counseling News, June 27, 2019, https://online.uwa.edu/news/emotional-psychology/.

13. *APA Dictionary of Psychology*, s.v. "complex emotion," https://dictionary.apa.org/complex-emotion.

14. Hokuma Karimova, "The Emotional Wheel: What It Is and How to Use It," Positive Psychology, December 24, 2017, https://positivepsychology.com/emotion-wheel.

15. T. S. Sathyanarayana et al., "The Biochemistry of Belief," *Indian Journal of Psychiatry* 51, no. 4 (2009): 239–41, https://www.ncbi.nlm.nih.gov/pmc/articles/PMC2802367/.

16. Matt Puderbaugh and Prabhu D. Emmady, *Neuroplasticity* (Treasure Island, FL: StatPearls, 2023), https://www.ncbi.nlm.nih.gov/books/NBK557811/.

17. Frontline, "How Much Do We Really Know About the Brain?," PBS, accessed May 7, 2024, https://www.pbs.org/wgbh/pages/frontline/shows/teenbrain/work/how.html.

18. Helen Shen, "Does the Adult Brain Really Grow New Neurons?" *Scientific American,* March 7, 2018, https://www.scientificamerican.com/article/does-the-adult-brain-really-grow-new-neurons/.

19. Saul Mcleod, "Maslow's Hierarchy of Needs," Simply Psychology, July 26, 2023, https://www.simplypsychology.org/maslow.html.

20. "5 Core Childhood Emotional Needs," Whole Self Therapy, March 26, 2019, https://wholeselftherapy.com/2019/03/26/5-core-childhood-emotional-needs/.

21. "The Helper: Enneagram Type Two," The Enneagram Institute, updated 2024, https://www.enneagraminstitute.com/type-2.

22. Catherine Moore, "What Is Negativity Bias and How Can It Be Overcome?," Positive Psychology, December 30, 2019, https://positivepsychology.com/3-steps-negativity-bias/.

23. Michael Bergeisen, "The Neuroscience of Happiness," *Greater Good Magazine*, September 22, 2010, https://greatergood.berkeley.edu/article/item/the_neuroscience_of_happiness.

24. Alexander J. Shackman and Tor D. Wager, "The Emotional Brain: Fundamental Questions and Strategies for Future Research," *Neuroscience Letters* 693, (2019): 68–74, https://www.ncbi.nlm.nih.gov/pmc/articles/PMC6370519/.

25. Simic et al., "Understanding Emotions."

26. Adam Rowden, "What to Know about Amygdala Hijack," *Medical News Today*, April 19, 2021, https://www.medicalnewstoday.com/articles/amygdala-hijack.

27. Kimberly Holland, "Amygdala Hijack: When Emotion Takes Over," Healthline, updated March 16, 2023, https://www.healthline.com/health/stress/amygdala-hijack.

28. This pattern is commonly known as the fight-or-flight pattern but technically is four responses: fight, flight, freeze, or please (or fawn). Some scientists also add a fifth response known as *flop*.

29. Martin Taylor, "What Does Fight, Flight, Freeze, Fawn Mean?," WebMD, April 28, 2022, https://www.webmd.com/mental-health/what-does-fight-flight-freeze-fawn-mean.

30. Oprah Winfrey and Bruce D. Perry, *What Happened to You? Conversations on Trauma, Resilience and Healing* (New York: Flatiron Books, 2021), 40.

Chapter 3 6 Truths about Emotions to Better Interpret All the Feels

1. See Exod. 22:24; 32:10; Num. 11:10; Gen. 6:6; Exod. 33:19; Deut. 30:3; Zeph. 2:7.

2. See Phil. 2:1; Luke 10:21; Rom. 5:5; 15:13.

3. See Matt. 23:1–15; John 11:35; Matt. 26:37–38; Luke 22:44.

4. See Numbers 14:1–12 for an example of God's people remaining in their own emotions instead of seeing God's provision in their lives.

5. Alicia Michelle and Lisa Appelo, "Episode 177: Coping with Grief and Shattering Loss When Tragedy Strikes with Lisa Appelo," *The Christian Mindset Coach with Alicia Michelle* (podcast), October 3, 2022, https://aliciamichelle.com/episode-177.

6. There's some debate as to who originally penned this quote. Many attribute it to famed psychologist, author, and Holocaust survivor Viktor Frankl, although there is no evidence of the quote in Frankl's writing.

7. Caroline Leaf, *Switch on Your Brain: The Key to Peak Happiness, Thinking and Health* (Grand Rapids: Baker Books, 2015), 66.

8. Gabor Maté and Daniel Maté, *The Myth of Normal: Trauma, Illness, and Healing in a Toxic Culture* (New York: Penguin Audio, 2022), 30:22.

9. Many credit this quote to Eleanor Roosevelt, and this article gives interesting evidence to that fact: "No One Can Make You Feel Inferior Without Your Consent," *Quote Investigator*, April 30, 2012, https://quoteinvestigator.com/2012/04/30/no-one-inferior/.

Chapter 4 Emotional Prep

1. Sarah Regan, "How to Use the Anger Iceberg to Work through Conflict & Emotions," MindBodyGreen, June 28, 2020, https://www.mindbodygreen.com/articles/the-anger-iceberg-and-how-to-work-with-it-effectively.

2. At the time of this printing there is debate about how much the amygdala is solely responsible for taking the logical brain offline, as in the case of the amygdala hijack. Some scientists argue that other brain structures such as the prefrontal cortex may also be responsible for how emotion takes over since this area of the brain helps us determine how to interpret situations. While scientists are still learning more about why emotions sometimes trump logical processing, it may be true that the amygdala and prefrontal cortex work in some sort of partnership to analyze in-the-moment emotions.

3. Dong Soon Oh, "Traumatic Experiences Disrupt Amygdala Prefrontal Connectivity," in *The Amygdala: A Discrete Multitasking Manager*, ed. Barbara Ferry (IntechOpen, 2012), https://www.intechopen.com/chapters/41582.

4. Murray B. Stein et al., "Increased Amygdala and Insult Activation during Emotion Processing in Anxiety-Prone Subjects," *The American Journal of Psychiatry* 164 (February 2007), https://ajp.psychiatryonline.org/doi/full/10.1176/ajp.2007.164.2.318#.

5. We realized later that, based on the mark in the dust of this man's car (yes, that's the extent of the "damage" we're talking about here), it was probably my door that hit his truck, so the man should have been directing his ire at me. It was God's grace that he didn't because I probably would have broken down in tears.

6. Elizabeth Coon, "Overview of the Autonomic Nervous System," *Merck Manual, Consumer Version*, July 2023, https://www.merckmanuals.com/home /brain,-spinal-cord,-and-nerve-disorders/autonomic-nervous-system-disorders /overview-of-the-autonomic-nervous-system.

7. Coon, "Overview of the Autonomic Nervous System."

8. Terry Hurtley, "Activating the Parasympathetic Nervous System to Decrease Stress and Anxiety," Canyon Vista Recovery Center, October 26, 2018, https:// canyonvista.com/activating-parasympathetic-nervous-system/.

9. Amanda Robb, "What Is the Parasympathetic Nervous System?," Study.com, accessed February 2, 2024, https://study.com/academy/lesson/parasympathetic -nervous-system-definition-function-effects.html.

10. Juan Murabe, "Hypotheses on the Development of Psychoemotional Tearing," *The Ocular Surface* 7, no. 4 (October 2009): 171, https://www.sciencedirect .com/sdfe/pdf/download/eid/1-s2.0-S1542012412701842/first-page-pdf.

11. Ashley Marcin, "9 Ways Crying May Benefit Your Health," Heathline, April 14, 2017, https://www.healthline.com/health/benefits-of-crying#detox.

12. Marla Paul, "Rhythm of Breathing Affects Memory and Fear," Neurosci enceNews.com, December 7, 2016, https://neurosciencenews.com/memory-fear -breathing-5699/.

13. Dana Santas, "Breathe Better to Live Better: Why Breathing Is Your Superpower," CNN, June 16, 2021, https://www.cnn.com/2021/06/16/health/breathing -better-training-wellness/index.html.

14. BetterHelp Editorial Team, "9 Visualization Techniques for Stress Reduction," BetterHelp, July 13, 2023, https://www.betterhelp.com/advice/stress /9-visualization-techniques-for-stress-reduction/.

15. Scott, "What Is a Highly Sensitive Person?"

16. Hope Gillette, "What to Know about Weighted Blankets and Autism," PsychCentral, September 29, 2021, https://psychcentral.com/autism/weighted -blankets-and-autism.

17. "Nurse Investigators on Using Weighted Blankets to Alleviate Anxiety during Cancer Treatment Infusions," Oncology Nursing News, April 30, 2023, https://www.oncnursingnews.com/view/nurse-investigators-on-using-weighted -blankets-to-alleviate-anxiety-during-cancer-treatment-infusions.

18. Gillette, "What to Know about Weighted Blankets and Autism."

19. Loren Toussaint et al., "Effectiveness of Progressive Muscle Relaxation, Deep Breathing and Guided Imagery in Promoting Psychological and Physiological States of Relaxation," *Evidence-based Complementary and Alternative Medicine* 2021, (July 2021), https://www.ncbi.nlm.nih.gov/pmc/articles/PMC8272667/.

20. Ralph Pawling et al., "C-Tactile Afferent Stimulating Touch Carries a Positive Affective Value," *PLoS One* 12, no. 3 (March 2017), https://www.ncbi.nlm .nih.gov/pmc/articles/PMC5345811/.

21. When considering which essential oils to use, choose those that offer a soothing smell and are also nonirritating should you choose to topically apply.

It's also wise to dilute any essential oils applied to the skin with a carrier liquid like coconut oil.

22. Apsorn Sattayakhom, Sineewanlaya Wichit, and Phanit Koomhin, "The Effects of Essential Oils on the Nervous System: A Scoping Review," *Molecules* 28, no. 9 (May 2023), https://www.ncbi.nlm.nih.gov/pmc/articles/PMC10180368/.

23. Michael Wotman et al., "The Efficacy of Lavender Aromatherapy in Reducing Preoperative Anxiety in Ambulatory Surgery Patients Undergoing Procedures in General Otolaryngology," *Investigative Otolaryngology* 2, no. 6 (December 2017), https://onlinelibrary.wiley.com/doi/full/10.1002/lio2.121.

24. Press Office, "Exercise and the Brain: The Neuroscience of Fitness Explored," NeuroscienceNews.com, May 13, 2023, https://neurosciencenews.com/fitness-neuroscience-23228/.

25. Amy Hale, "Can We Change Ourselves Simply by Changing Location?" *Psychology Today*, February 8, 2012, https://www.psychologytoday.com/us/blog/the-power-places/201202/can-we-change-ourselves-simply-changing-location.

26. Rich Co, "Enjoying Nature, Green, Blue Spaces Reduces Prescription Drug Needs for Mental Health, Study Shows," *Nature World News*, January 18, 2023, https://www.natureworldnews.com/articles/55096/20230118/enjoying-nature-green-blue-spaces-reduces-prescription-drug-needs-mental.htm.

27. Christian Heiser, "What the Beach Does to Your Brain," *Better by Today*, July 15, 2018, https://www.nbcnews.com/better/health/what-beach-does-your-brain-ncna787231.

28. Amanda MacMillan, "Why Nature Sounds Are Great for Relaxation," Health, June 13, 2022, https://www.health.com/condition/stress/why-nature-sounds-are-relaxing.

29. Sonja Aalbers et al., "Music Therapy for Depression," *Cochrane Database of Systematic Reviews 2017*, no. 11 (November 2017), https://doi.org/10.1002/14651858.CD004517.pub3; Joke Bradt, Cheryl Dileo, and Noah Potvin, "Music for Stress and Anxiety Reduction in Coronary Heart Disease Patients," *Cochrane Database of Systematic Reviews 2013*, no. 12 (December 2013), https://doi.org/10.1002/14651858.CD006577.pub3.

30. Bradt, Dileo, and Potvin, "Music for Stress and Anxiety Reduction."

31. Alicia Michelle and Katrina Sequenzia, "Episode 207: Wait . . . Emotional Eating Can Be OK? with Katrina Sequenzia," *The Christian Mindset Coach with Alicia Michelle* (podcast), May 1, 2023, https://aliciamichelle.com/episode-207.

Chapter 6 A Is for Acknowledge

1. Harry Sherrin, "Benjamin Guggenheim: The Titanic Victim Who Went Down 'Like a Gentleman,'" History Hit, April 9, 2022, https://www.historyhit.com/benjamin-guggenheim-the-titanic-victim-who-died-like-a-gentleman/.

2. Jen Wilkin, "Week 2 Video Teaching," *God of Creation: A Study of Genesis 1–11,* Nashville: Lifeway Press, 2021.

3. Sian Ferguson, "Breaking the Cycle of Shame and Self-Destructive Behavior," Psych Central, October 21, 2022, https://psychcentral.com/lib/breaking-the-cycle-of-shame-and-self-destructive-behavior.

4. Katherine Wolf, Instagram post on @HopeHeals, September 22, 2023, https://www.instagram.com/p/CxgG59SLct1/.

5. "How Do We Know the Angel of the Lord Is Jesus?," Verse by Verse Ministry International, February 2, 2016, https://versebyverseministry.org/bible-answers /how-do-we-know-the-angel-of-the-lord-is-jesus.

6. Alyson M. Stone, "90 Seconds to Emotional Resilience," AlysonMStone .com, November 19, 2019, https://www.alysonmstone.com/90-seconds-to-emo tional-resilience/.

7. Proverbs 15:4 describes gentle words as a "tree of life" and says a deceitful tongue crushes the spirit. We read in John 6:63 and John 6:68 that Jesus's words give eternal life. Acts 7:38 speaks of how Moses received life-giving words from the angel at Mount Sinai that he passed on to the people.

8. Maria Richter et al., "Do Words Hurt? Brain Activation During the Processing of Pain-Related Words," *Pain* 148, no. 2 (February 2010): 177–354, https://doi .org/10.1016/j.pain.2009.08.009.

9. Andrew Newber, *Words Can Change Your Brain* (New York: Avery, 2012), as quoted by Lindsey Horton in "The Neuroscience Behind Our Words," BRM Institute, August 8, 2019, https://brm.institute/neuroscience-behind-words.

10. Alicia Michelle and Nancy Hicks, "Episode 140: How to Mentally Prepare for the Holiday Season without a Loved One with Nancy Hicks," *The Christian Mindset Coach with Alicia Michelle* (podcast), November 9, 2021, https:// aliciamichelle.com/episode-140.

11. Philippians 4:8 calls us to fix our thoughts on "whatever is true, whatever is noble, whatever is right, whatever is pure, whatever is lovely, whatever is admirable." This action comes *after* we've presented our fears and worries to God and allowed the peace of God to enter our minds as noted in Philippians 4:6–7, however. We're called to process the pain *before* focusing on the good.

12. Peace doesn't hide dysfunction but makes space for frustrations to be safely processed within a loving relationship. More on this in a later chapter when we talk about emotional boundaries.

13. Stuart Wolpert, "Putting Feelings into Words Produces Therapeutic Effects in the Brain; UCLA Neuroimaging Study Supports Ancient Buddhist Teachings," UCLA Newsroom, June 21, 2007, https://newsroom.ucla.edu/releases/Putting -Feelings-Into-Words-Produces-8047.

Chapter 7 D Is for Discern

1. Alicia Michelle, "Episode 110: Conviction vs. Condemnation: What's the Difference?" *The Christian Mindset Coach with Alicia Michelle* (podcast), March 29, 2021, https://aliciamichelle.com/episode-110.

2. Adam Macinnis, "Report: 26 Million Americans Stopped Reading the Bible Regularly During COVID," *Christianity Today*, April 20, 2022, https:// www.christianitytoday.com/news/2022/april/state-of-bible-reading-decline-report -26-million.html.

3. Alicia Michelle, "Episode 200: Transformation Story: How Bryn Found Healing from Crippling Anxiety," *The Christian Mindset Coach with Alicia Michelle* (podcast), March 13, 2023, https://aliciamichelle.com/episode-200.

4. Madelyn Brown, "What Radical Acceptance Really Means," Psych Central, March 31, 2022, https://psychcentral.com/blog/what-it-really-means-to-practice -radical-acceptance.

Chapter 8 D Is for Decide

1. Alicia Michelle and Melissa Ferguson, "Episode 213: Deciding to Obey God + Believe in His Goodness Despite Cancer with Melissa Ferguson," *The Christian Mindset Coach with Alicia Michelle* (podcast), June 12, 2023, https://aliciamichelle.com/episode-213.

2. Emily Nagosoki and Amelia Nagosoki, *Burnout: The Secret to Unlocking the Stress Cycle* (New York: Penguin Random House Audio, 2019), 47:51.

Chapter 9 Anger

1. Galatians 5:19–21 also describes "outbursts of anger," not anger itself, as part of the list of the desires of the sinful nature.

Chapter 10 Disappointment

1. Kayleigh Roberts, "The Queen Once Said 'Grief Is the Price We Pay for Love,'" *Marie Claire*, April 18, 2021, https://www.marieclaire.com/celebrity/a36153127/queen-said-grief-is-the-price-we-pay-for-love/.

Chapter 13 Discontentment

1. See the story of God's provision of manna for the Israelites in Exodus 16:11–26. God told them to take what they needed, and some took more because they had a bigger family. On the day before Sabbath God told them to take more so they wouldn't have to work on the Sabbath, and He rained down the perfect amount of manna each day that fully met each person's needs for provision.

Chapter 14 Loneliness

1. Center for Disease Control Media Relations, "New CDC Data Illuminate Youth Mental Health Threats During the COVID-19 Pandemic," CDC Press Release, March 31, 2022, https://www.cdc.gov/media/releases/2022/p0331-youth-mental-health-covid-19.html.

2. U.S. Surgeon General, "Our Epidemic of Loneliness and Isolation."

3. Michael Gryboski, "Universities Nationwide Experiencing 'A Spirit of Unity and Confession' Spurred by Asbury Revival," *The Christian Post*, February 21, 2023, https://www.christianpost.com/news/asbury-revival-spreading-to-more-universities-churches.html.

4. Since a lack of self-care can greatly alter our ability to process our emotions and to accurately ascertain the health of our relationships, we've included these questions to help you determine if ministering to these basic health needs could potentially improve the depth of any feelings of loneliness.

Chapter 16 Using ADD to Better Manage Emotions in Relationships

1. Tony Miltenberger, conference session, "Don't Believe Your Own Hype: Staying Committed to Your Identity in Christ," Spark Media Ignite Conference, September 30, 2023.

Chapter 17 Habits and Next Steps for Ongoing Emotional Confidence

1. Eti Ben Simon, "Why Just One Sleepless Night Makes People Emotionally Fragile," *Scientific American*, August 15, 2023, https://www.scientificamerican.com/article/why-just-one-sleepless-night-makes-people-emotionally-fragile/.

2. University of York, "High-Quality Sleep Promotes Resilience to Depression and Anxiety," Science Daily, July 13, 2023, https://www.sciencedaily.com/releases/2023/07/230713141922.htm.

3. Eti Ben Simon et al., "Sleep Loss and the Socio-Emotional Brain," *Trends in Cognitive Science* 24, no.6 (April 2020): 435–50, https://pubmed.ncbi.nlm.nih.gov/32299657/.

4. Sue Penckofer et al., "Does Glycemic Variability Impact Mood and Quality of Life?," *Diabetes Technology and Therapeutics* 14, no. 4 (April 2012): 303–310, https://www.ncbi.nlm.nih.gov/pmc/articles/PMC3317401/.

5. Johns Hopkins Medicine, "The Brain-Gut Connection," *Hopkins Medicine*, accessed May 9, 2024, https://www.hopkinsmedicine.org/health/wellness-and-prevention/the-brain-gut-connection.

6. Marta Zaraska, "Want to Improve Your Mental Health? Eat Your Greens," *Washington Post*, May 23, 2023, https://www.washingtonpost.com/wellness/2023/05/23/vegetables-fruit-mental-health/; Katharine Lang, "Ultra-Processed Foods May Increase Depression Risk, Long-Term Study Shows," Medical News Today, May 22, 2023, https://www.medicalnewstoday.com/articles/ultra-processed-foods-may-increase-depression-risk-long-term-study-shows#1.

7. "Can Menopause Cause Depression?," Hopkins Medicine, accessed April 16, 2024, https://www.hopkinsmedicine.org/health/wellness-and-prevention/can-menopause-cause-depression.

8. "Can Menopause Cause Depression?"

9. "Serotonin," Cleveland Clinic, March 18, 2022, https://health.clevelandclinic.org/hormone-testing.

10. Ashish Sharma, Vishal Madaan, and Frederick D. Petty, "Exercise for Mental Health," *The Primary Care Companion to the Journal of Clinical Psychiatry* 8, no. 6 (2006): 106, https://www.ncbi.nlm.nih.gov/pmc/articles/PMC1470658/.

11. Ben Singh et al., "Effectiveness of Physical Activity Interventions for Improving Depression, Anxiety and Distress: An Overview of Systematic Reviews," *British Journal of Sports Medicine* 57, (February 2023), https://bjsm.bmj.com/content/early/2023/07/11/bjsports-2022-106195.

12. Sharma, Madaan, and Petty, "Exercise for Mental Health."

About the Author

Alicia Michelle, ACC, CPLC, is an ICF-certified Christian life coach and NeuroCoach, a popular conference speaker, and the multi-award-winning host of the top-ranked podcast *The Christian Mindset Coach with Alicia Michelle*. Through her coaching and courses, Alicia has equipped tens of thousands of women with practical brain-science-and-Bible-based tools to better manage emotions and to break free from perfectionism and people-pleasing in order to cultivate Christ-centered confidence. She loves to travel, cook, paint, and enjoy life with her beloved husband, four kids, and four dogs. Learn more and download free resources at AliciaMichelle.com.

Connect with Alicia:

AliciaMichelle.com

f @AliciaMichelleCoach

📷 @AliciaMichelleCoach

▶ @AliciaMichelleCoach